"*Of all the blithesome melody*
That makes the warm heart thrill,
Give me the wind that whistles free
Across the moorland hill;
When every blade upon the lea
Is dancing with delight,
And every bush and flower and tree
Is singing in its flight ..."

- Edwin Waugh
(The Moorland Breeze)

Front Cover
Thorpe Cloud from Bunster Hill
(Walk 34, Sept 10)
Previous Page
Ladder stile near White Hall
(Walk 24, Dec 12)
This Title Page
Peter's Stone, Cressbrook Dale
(Walk 39, May 9)
Title Page Right
Approaching Mother Cap
(Walk 22, Aug 27)

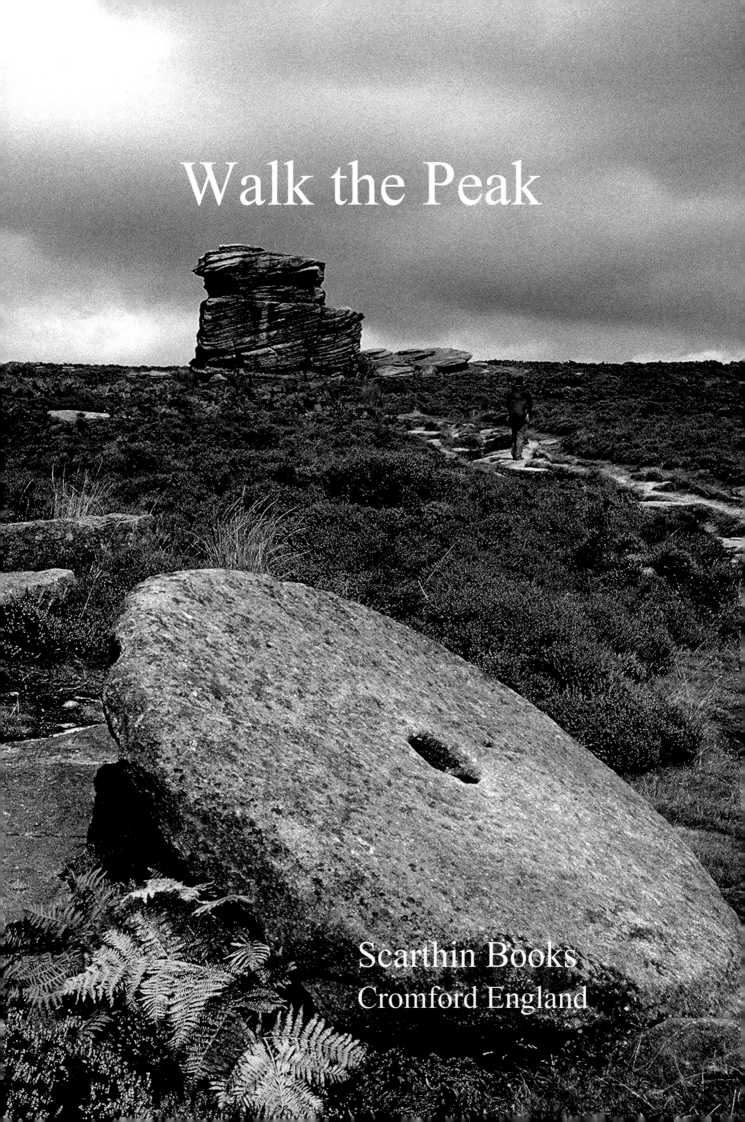

Walk the Peak

Scarthin Books
Cromford England

Howden Dam and the Upper Derwent
(Nov 15)

Scarthin Books, Cromford,
Derbyshire DE4 3QF, UK. (01629 823272)
www.scarthinbooks.com

Printed in China by 1010 Printing International Ltd

Walk The Peak
Copyright © Rod Dunn, 2007

ISBN 9781900446112

Disclaimer
Like most outdoor activities, walking and scrambling can be hazardous and are done entirely at you own risk. As well as the terrain, other dangers may include the weather; animals; landslip; rock-fall; other outdoor pursuits participants and road vehicles. The publisher, the author or the landowner(s) are not liable for any injuries or loss of life to first or third parties or responsible for the loss or damage to first or third person property or equipment or losing one's direction and incurring any discomfort or expense whatsoever whilst on any of the walks in this publication or taking any of the advice or acting on other information contained so herein.

Always err on the side of caution. The dales, hills and crags will be there for another day - make sure you are.

In An Emergency
Dial 999 and ask for police and mountain rescue. Give your location as exact as possible together with the suspected injuries of the casualty. If phoning from a mobile, keep the phone switched on. See also page 34.

Note The ozone layer over northern Europe is now much depleted and skin cancer is on the increase. If you're going to be outside for extended periods cover up and use sunblock.

An autumn storm over Higger Tor (left) and Carl Wark hill fort (Walk 22, Oct 26)

Map of The Peak District National Park (and environs)

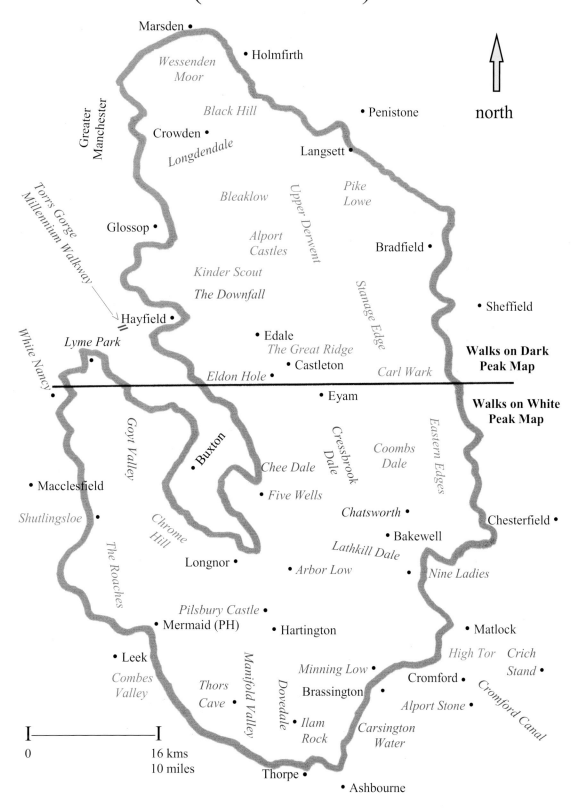

Marsden •

• Holmfirth

Wessenden Moor

Black Hill

Greater Manchester

Crowden •

• Penistone   north

Longdendale

Langsett •

Torrs Gorge Millennium Walkway

Bleaklow

Upper Derwent

Pike Lowe

Glossop •

Alport Castles

Bradfield •

Kinder Scout

The Downfall

Stanage Edge

White Nancy

Hayfield •

• Sheffield

Lyme Park

• Edale

The Great Ridge

Walks on Dark Peak Map

Eldon Hole •

• Castleton

Carl Wark

• Eyam

Walks on White Peak Map

Goyt Valley

• Buxton

Cressbrook Dale

Coombs Dale

Eastern Edges

Chee Dale

• Macclesfield

Five Wells

Shutlingsloe •

Chatsworth •

Chesterfield •

Chrome Hill

• Bakewell

The Roaches

Lathkill Dale

Longnor •

• *Arbor Low*

• *Nine Ladies*

Pilsbury Castle •

• Matlock

• Mermaid (PH)

• Hartington

High Tor   *Crich Stand* •

• Leek

Minning Low •

Cromford •

Combes Valley

Thors Cave

Manifold Valley

Dovedale

Brassington

Alport Stone •

Cromford Canal

• *Ilam Rock*

Carsington Water

0 ——————— 16 kms
              10 miles

Thorpe •

• Ashbourne

Contents

Natural floral display at Hobs House (Walk 41, May 15)

On the buttercup-clad ridge and furrow fields beneath Rainster Rocks (Walk 49, June 2)

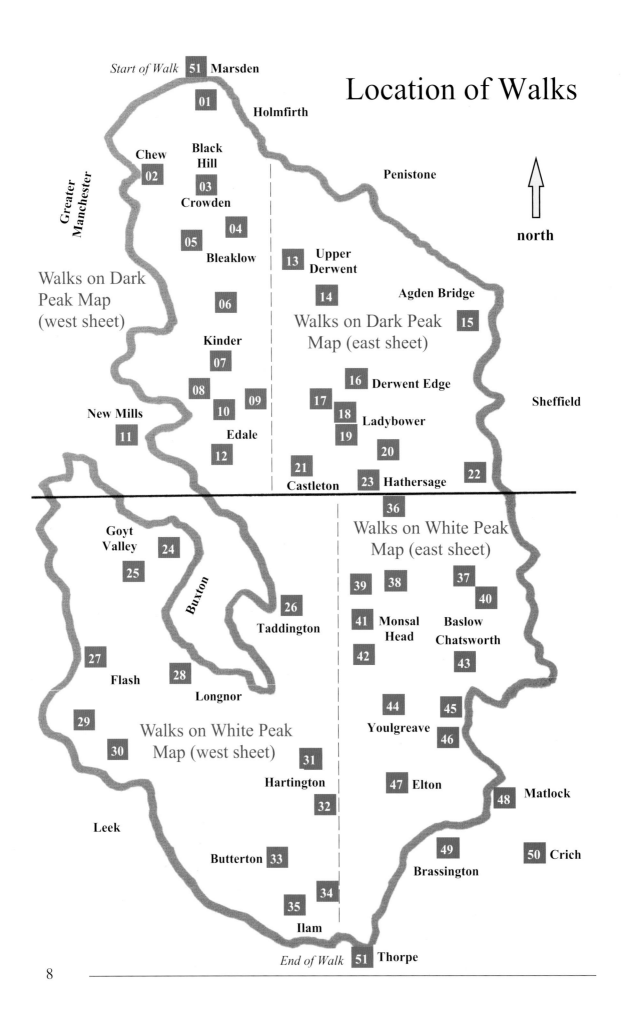

Location of Walks

Start of Walk 51 Marsden

01

Holmfirth

Chew
02

Black
Hill
03

Crowden

Greater Manchester

04

05

Bleaklow

13 Upper
Derwent

14

Agden Bridge

15

Walks on Dark
Peak Map
(west sheet)

06

Walks on Dark Peak
Map (east sheet)

Kinder
07

16 Derwent Edge

08

17

Sheffield

New Mills

10   09

18
19 Ladybower

11

Edale
12

20

21

23 Hathersage   22

Castleton

36

Goyt
Valley   24

Walks on White Peak
Map (east sheet)

25

39   38

37
40

Buxton

26

41 Monsal
Head

Baslow
Chatsworth

Taddington

42

43

27

28

44

45

Flash

Longnor

Youlgreave

46

29

Walks on White Peak
Map (west sheet)

47 Elton

30

31

48 Matlock

Hartington

32

Leek

49

50 Crich

Butterton 33

Brassington

35

34

Ilam

End of Walk 51 Thorpe

north

Introduction

So many words have been written about Britain's first National Park and its environs, that it is almost impossible to come up with an original introduction to "The Peak", as the Peak District is affectionately known to its aficionados. The *New Oxford Dictionary of English* defines the Peak District as "a limestone plateau in Derbyshire at the southern end of the Pennines rising to 636m at Kinder Scout". Well *that's* original - but quite wrong. True, there is a limestone plateau in The Peak, but this reaches beyond Derbyshire into Staffordshire and has been eroded by rivers past and present into the dales, gorges and caves we see today. The tops of many hills on the limestone were chosen as burial sites by our ancestors, but these hills fall a couple of hundred metres short of Kinder, which lies in the huge area of Millstone grit, shale grit and shale which surrounds the Carboniferous limestone, and expands from Derbyshire into Staffordshire, Cheshire, South and West Yorkshire and Greater Manchester. These rocks give rise to the Edges and surrounding heather moors; outcrops such as Black Rocks and The Roaches and, in the north of the region, the high blanket bogs of peat on Bleaklow, Kinder, Black Hill and Wessenden. There are also coal measures and younger rocks on the flanks of The Peak.

It is often written that The Peak is the most visited of all our National Parks. One reason is certainly its location, encircled as it is by conurbations, whose denizens arrive in droves on Sundays and Bank Holidays. But there is another reason for such popularity. Literary historians lauded The Peak's wonders and cursed its bleakness - and, herein, lies the answer - diversity. No other National Park can offer such a variety of scenery. As well as these landscapes, the flora and fauna are also governed by the geology, with the limestone dales having the richest assemblages. Here, the sunnier south face of a dale may support totally different plant species to the north side, and the scree, cliff ledges and spoil-heaps from old leadmines harbour their own specialities. Many of these dales are National Nature Reserves, managed by English Nature. The limestone area is often referred to as The White Peak. Scenery on the grit, sandstone and shale is known as The Dark Peak, and supports different species to the limestone. Red grouse are prevalent on the heather, but the adder and insectivorous sundew are scarce on the heaths. The higher blanket bogs are the domain of the mountain hare, cloudberry and the summer-visiting golden plover. The peregrine falcon again has dominion of the sky. Some of the rocks on these high places have been eroded into fantastic shapes. Around quarries now frequented by rock-climbers lie many of the abandoned millstones from which the Peak District National Park takes its emblem. The mass trespass over Kinder Scout in 1932 may have led to access agreements which we enjoy today. Over 50 reservoirs add to the attraction of the Dark Peak. Some rivers in the White Peak are legendary for fly-fishing and many haunting sites from prehistory remain etched in the landscape. We are fortunate that the National Trust owns most of The Peak's gems, and Wildlife Trusts and the National Park Authority others. Some paths on popular routes are indeed eroded, but even countless boots cannot compete with the damage caused by the elements, acid rain and overgrazing. Hence, I make no excuses for including them. Most walkers are sympathetic to the Countryside Code; others are litter-louts, and some selfish ramblers' groups arrive individually and monopolise car parks. So early starts are recommended. These, then, are my 50 favourite walks through this diverse and unique landscape. But before you pack the rucksacks and set off, here is a (largely) pictorial introduction for those of you unfamiliar with this oasis in the middle of urban England ...

White Peak Scenery The limestone of the dales, crags and plateaux, largely formed from the remains of unimaginable numbers of sea creatures eons ago, had already been subjected to glaciation, folding, volcanic activity and erosion before humans added to the scene by mining, deforesting, quarrying and farming. **Top.** *The short but spectacular Winnats Pass near Castleton is visited on walk 21.* **Bottom.** *Dolomitic limestone pinnacle near Longcliffe (SK 224 554, May 14). There are some wonderful rock formations in this area, which is sadly not in the National Park. Many of the outcrops are seen on Walk 49.*

*Walking through upper Lathkill Dale (Walk 44, May 11). Here, flowers such as Jacob's ladder, crosswort, dark mullein and, dropwort (**Inset**), flourish in late June.*

Dark Peak Scenery Gritstone, shale and blanket bog have been eroded by the elements and geologically manipulated over the millennia. Man, too, has influenced the landscape by over-grazing sheep, quarrying, cutting down the forests and contributing to acid rainfall via industry. This has, however, left us with some spectacular and challenging terrain to enjoy. On Bleaklow, Kinder Scout and other blanket bogs there are many groughs (pron. "groffs"). These are channels, some as much as 4 metres deep, formed by watercourses eroding peat down to bedrock. Skilled walkers use them to navigate their way through boggy areas. **Top.** *Walking through a grough on Bleaklow (Walk 6, July 11).* **Bottom.** *Formations such as the Crow Stones are testament to the ferocious weather the high places have endured over the millennia (Walk 13, Aug 16).*

Fair Brook provides a lovely ascent of Kinder Scout (Walk 7, Aug 16). As well as ling and bell heather (the food plants of red grouse and emperor moth larvae), other plants on the blanket bog include cross-leaved heath, cloudberry, cottongrass, cowberry, bog sedges and crowberry. Kinder Scout is internationally recognised as a unique mountain habitat. To be involved in Peak moorland conservation visit www.moorsforthefuture.org.uk

The Underground Peak Watercourses and fissures in some limestone areas have been eroded and dissolved over the millennia into caves and potholes - some vast, some tiny, and some with wonderful formations due to mineral deposition. The caves and mines of The Peak also provide roosts for several species of bat. **Top.** *A (very) trusting lady peers into the depths of Eldon Hole (SK 117 808). First explored in 1780, it was the deepest pothole in The Peak at 82m until Titan, twice as deep, was discovered in 2006 (p.118).* **Bottom.** *Poole's Cavern in Buxton (SK 050 726) has some of the best formations of any show cave in The Peak with* **left**, *flowstone, a calcite deposition, and* **right**, *the Poached Egg Chamber! There is also an exhibition of cave photographs and fossils at the site.*

Top. *At the entrance to Thirst House Cave in Deep Dale (SK 097 712). A torch reveals two chambers with very uneven floors - formed by the compressed debris of archaeological excavations.* **Right Inset.** *In the roof of the first chamber are a series of similar carvings. Their shape suggests ancient fertility symbols. This example was photographed on 07/11/04.* **Left Inset.** *There is a healthy population of the impressive cave spider, too!* **Bottom.** *Nan Tor Cave at Wetton Mill has yielded human occupation remains from the Mesolithic and animals from a glacial period, including arctic fox and lemmings (Walk 33, Sept 23).* **Inset.** *Hibernating long-eared bat (Feb 5). Herald moths, peacock and small tortoiseshell butterflies also see out the winter in some Peak caves, adits and mines.*

Reservoirs There are over 50 reservoirs in the Peak District and some of them, particularly those of the Upper Derwent, Longdendale and Greenfield areas, are reminiscent of the Lake District. **Top.** *Dovestone Reservoir and Alderman's Hill from the track to Chew Reservoir, which is the highest in England (Walk 2, Aug 31).* **Bottom.** *Overflowing Howden Dam and Reservoir seen from Abbey Bank (Walk 16, Nov 15). Howden and Derwent Reservoirs were used by the crew of 617 Squadron to train for the famous dam-busting runs to the Moehne and Eder Dams in the Ruhr Valley in 1943. The dams of the Upper Derwent were also used as locations for the film, "The Dambusters".*

Fossils You will see many fossils as you walk in the White Peak. Limestone walls and stiles and steps polished by many boots are good places to look, and some natural outcrops have fine examples. Crinoids, an ancient sea-lily, are frequently seen and polish up to resemble nuts and bolts. **Top.** *The crags at Stoney Middleton (SK 223 757) have many fossils (and wallflowers, May 7). Beneath the crags, the roof of Oyster Passage in Carlswark Cavern is adorned with unique bivalves.* **Bottom Left.** *Hobs House in Monsal Dale (Walk 41) is a Site of Special Scientific Interest (SSSI) for its strata of species' extinctions and emergences.* **Bottom Right.** *Fist-sized brachiopod in wall approaching Alport near the end of Walk 44.* (To see crinoidal outcrops, treat yourself to Walk 39!).

Neolithic Sites There are many haunting sites left by early settlers in The Peak. Unfortunately, most of them were crudely excavated by Victorian antiquarians. Our ancestors were laid to rest with such reverence that one has to question the ethics of such antics for brief public acclaim and academic kudos. It is, simply, grave-robbing.

Top. *The 17 ancient beech trees on the chambered barrow of Minning Low (SK 209 572, June 21) are visible from many walks.* **Bottom Right.** *The megalithic barrow of Five Wells (SK 123 710) is best reached from Chelmorton (footpath left of church).* **Bottom Left.** *Rock art replica near Gardom's Edge (Walk 40, Aug 19). But is it ceremonial art, doodling or could it even be a means of counting? It is interesting that there are ten small holes in each of two larger circles. By adding pebbles as counters to these and other rings a stone abacus could easily be made. We encounter other rock art on walks 36 and 46, and there are examples at Ashover (school) and at Sheffield Museum from a find above Bakewell. But one has to wonder how the engravings survived 5,000 years of weathering.*

Top. *Arbor Low henge is regarded as the "Stonehenge of The North" (SK 160 635, July 22). It is not known whether the stones were laid flat or fell. The Bull Ring henge at Dove Holes has no stones at all (SK 078 782).* **Middle.** *The Seven Stones of Hordron circle lies south of Cutthroat Bridge on Hordron Edge at SK 215 868. This most evocative of Peak stone circles enjoys expansive views to Winhill and beyond.* **Bottom.** *There are 4 remaining stones to Nine Stones circle on Harthill Moor (Walk 46, Oct 12). It is documented that six were standing in 1860, but they made ideal gateposts, too!*

The Magpie Mine was constructed using the proven design of Cornish tin and copper mines.

The Mining Legacy There are many relics of lead and copper mining to be seen in the limestone landscape. Many sites now support interesting wild flowers on the old spoil heaps and rakes (mineral veins), some of which have been reworked for fluorspar. The ancient mines, hell to work in, now provide sporting trips for experienced cavers. **Top.** *The Magpie Mine is visited on Walk 42 (May 30).* **Bottom Left.** *The traditional beehiveshaped mineshaft caps are fast disappearing to repair nearby dry stone walls. This (to date) surviving example is near Wardlow Mires at SK 191 758.* **Bottom Right.** *Metal-rich spoil-heaps support their own flora such as spring sandwort, alpine penny-cress and, here, beside a footpath near Brightgate at SK 257 596, mountain pansies (May 12).*

The Quarrying Legacy Millstones (now the emblem of the National Park), along with grindstones, have been quarried in The Peak since the mid 15th century, and hundreds remain abandoned after cheaper foreign imports sealed the fate of the industry. For some reason, pinnacles were left standing at several gritstone quarries. These days, it is limestone which is in great demand, and many quarry faces scar the landscape. However, nature eventually returns, and interesting plants such as bee orchid, dark red helleborine and twayblade may colonise the stony ground. Climbers, too, enjoy the sheer rock faces of abandoned limestone and gritstone quarries. **Top left.** *The Alport Stone near Wirksworth is the sentinel of the area, presiding over the flatlands to the south (SK 302 517, May 23). Nearby, at Alport Heights, there is a toposcope and CP.* **Top right.** *Bee orchid growing in a disused limestone quarry at Millers Dale (SK 138 730, June 21).* **Bottom.** *A few of the hundreds of millstones that lay beneath the Surprise Corner (SK 248 800, Oct 25). Some bear the initials of the stonemasons, including those of my great-grandfather who was killed when a maverick horse with a cart of millstones ran amok.*

The Environment Top. *Common cotton-grass and rushes flourish in the bogs beneath Stanage Edge, but bracken has ousted the heather and moor grasses from the drier slopes (Walk 20, July 9). Regular burning (as on grouse moors) and re-seeding would return many areas to their former glory.* **Centre Left.** *Set-aside policies have led to grass monoculture being replaced by herb-rich fields, such as this ox-eye daisy meadow near Darwin Lake at SK 305 644 (June 18).* **Centre Right.** *Although they receive grants and subsidies to look after their land, some farmers persist in illegal fly-tipping. This eyesore is beside a footpath on Walk 32. Tractors and farm machinery are left to rot at many farms, and it is a joke to anoint these landowners as "Custodians Of The Countryside".* **Bottom.** *It may be pretty when in flower, but invasive Himalayan balsam has ousted many indigenous plant species (Walk 11, Sept 14).*

Chimneys Old and New Top. *The oldest surviving industrial chimney in Britain (c1770) has been restored and may be visited via a footpath at Stone Edge (SK 335 669). It was once part of a lead smelting site (Aug 17).* **Bottom Left.** *Leawood Pump House on the Cromford Canal (SK 315 557) is part of the chain of World Heritage listed sites between Matlock and Belper (May 22).* **Bottom Right.** *The colossal 130 metre high chimney of the cement works at Pindale, seen here from above Castleton at Dirt Low (SK 157 823), towers out of the mist and dominates the Hope Valley from afar (Jan 20).*

Recreation The Peak District, with its abundance of caves, crags, hills, dales, rivers and reservoirs is tailor-made for many outdoor activities. **Top.** *Hang-gliding off Sugworth Edge, near Boots Folly (SK 232 898, Oct 28). The folly was erected in 1927 by unemployed local men to find them work during a depression. A fine gesture by the landowner in austere times.* **Bottom Left.** *A fly-fisherman tries his luck on the River Wye at Upperdale (Walk 41, June 10). Rivers such as The Wye, Dove and Lathkill are legendary for their fishing, a pastime also popular on the reservoirs. However, anglers have no more right to fish than goosanders and cormorants, which are being illegally shot.* **Bottom Right.** *When fully frozen, Kinder Downfall hones ice-climbing skills (Walk 10, Dec 30).*

Top. *Pony-trekkers on the path between Win Hill and Hope Cross (Walk 19, Oct 5). The group almost provide a toposcope of the view : Lose Hill is above the 1st rider; Rushup Edge the 2nd; The Vale of Edale is between the 3rd and 4th riders and Kinder Scout is just coming into view above the last rider. A local legend claims that Lose Hill and Win Hill were named by the winners and losers following a battle fought in prehistory. Hmm.*

Middle. *A canoeist on the short stretch of white water on the River Derwent at Matlock Bath (SK 297 585, Oct 22). This is one of the few waterways on which canoeing is permitted. Canoeists cause less damage to fish habitats than do anglers' feet and they should be given access to more water in The Peak and throughout Britain.*

Bottom. *Sailing on Dovestone Reservoir (Walk 2, Aug 3). Sailing, wind-surfing and canoeing tuition are on offer at Carsington Water (Walk 49), but most reservoirs are the preserve of clubs or anglers.*

Floods, Fires and Foot and Mouth With the weather now unpredictable, floods and fires occur in The Peak at unseasonable times. The spring drought in 2003 saw fires for over a week on Bleaklow and Kinder Scout, as plants burnt and peat smouldered. In 2002, torrential rain in August was so relentless that the waterlogged ground could absorb no more, and the run-off led to landslides and swollen brooks hurtling thousands of tons of stones and debris downstream. In November 2000, the river levels were already high and exceptional rainfall led to fluvial flooding of the lower Derwent Valley. The national foot and mouth outbreak in the winter of 2001 saw footpaths and access land closed to walkers, who then rambled the lanes. **Top.** *The flooded Derwent Valley between Rowsley and Matlock (Nov 6, 2000).* **Bottom.** *Wetton Hills from Wetton Road, taken during the national foot and mouth outbreak that fortunately didn't reach The Peak (March 3, 2001).*

Waterfalls We visit most of the notable waterfalls on our journey through The Peak. (See page 241 for some falls not on the walks). **Above.** *Birchen Clough (Walk 2, Aug 3).*

Farming Traditional farming largely prevails throughout The Peak, but new livestock breeds and crops such as maize are being introduced. **Top.** *Protective parents near Litton (Walk 39, May 9).* **Middle.** *It could be South America, but this farm is at Ridge Head (SK 038 644).* **Bottom.** *Open barn with dew pond that has been allowed to mature (Walk 39, May 9). There is an abundance of wildlife at such sites; swallows and blackbirds nest inside the barn; pied wagtails and blue tits in the outer walls. Weasels frequent the dry stone walls and the pond supports frogs, newts, dragonflies and damselflies, whirligig beetles, water boatmen and other bugs, as well as broad-leaved pond-weed and starwort.*

Top. *Cows enjoying a buttercup meadow in Monsal Dale (Walk 41, June 21), unaware that more robust breeds such as longhorns, water-buffalo and belted Galloway, seen here,* **Middle,** *at Castleton, are beginning to interest more upland farmers.* **Bottom.** *The traditional haystacks and hayricks have long since been replaced with the ubiquitous, but still photogenic roll, that is, until they are heaped together wrapped in garish plastic.*

However, farming is not always so idyllic. Some farms in the National Park are little more than scrap-yards, where livestock huddle together knee-deep in excrement and mud. This is a local and national disgrace.

Rock Climbing was born on the edges and crags of the Peak District by a few hard pioneers from the Sheffield and Manchester areas. Successive generations forge harder routes using techniques and aids that some purists frown upon. This means that classic ascents such as *The Peapod* on Curbar Edge (**above**) are seldom attempted these days.

Walls and Gate Posts There are thousands of miles of dry stone walls in The Peak. In the White Peak, the limestone walls tend to be maintained due to grants, but many gritstone and sandstone walls in the Dark Peak will never rise again. Once a dying skill, the art of repairing and building dry stone walls is now undergoing a renaissance. Many standing stones and guide posts (or stoops) were uprooted by the landowners for farm gate posts. Many of the stoops had directions to four destinations inscribed on the faces in dialectal spelling. There is now a society pledged to return the stoops to their original sites. **Top.** *Above Milldale looking towards the miles of limestone walls around Alstonefield (Walk 32, Dec 10).* **Bottom Left.** *The pastel shades of sandstone near Hanging Rock Farm soon weather to a dark brown (Walk 29, Jan 25).* **Bottom Right**. *A fine guide stoop used as a gate post at a farm above Two Dales (SK 285 634, June 22).*

Aircraft Wrecks Sadly, more than 50 aircraft have come down in The Peak. Most crashes occurred in the Dark Peak during, or just after, World War II. Even though they had radar, many pilots flew "by their pants", but some were caught out when sudden mists or low cloud obscured high ground. Other crashes were inexplicable mid-air collisions or due to faulty equipment. Some crews survived the crashes, but many perished, and we should treat the crash sites with respect. We visit 13 different crash sites on our walks. The wreckage from lower altitude crashes such as those at Foolow and near Beeley Moor were removed. **Left.** *Engine remains from the two Sabre F86 jets which collided in mid-air over Black Ashop Moor in 1954 (Walk 7, Aug 11). Both pilots perished.* **Below.** *Remains of the Stirling LJ628 which came down near Upper Commons in 1944. The crew of ten survived and two of the least injured walked miles across very rough terrain for help (Walk 14, Aug 27).*

Rivers, Ponds and Meres Some rivers that flow over limestone, such as The Manifold and the upper reaches of The Lathkill, disappear underground during droughts. After heavy rain, resurgent spouts may suddenly erupt from fissures in the dry river beds. A good place to see this phenomenon is on the River Manifold just south of Ecton. To counteract the paucity of standing water on the limestone plateau, meres and dew ponds (p.28) were constructed on the porous limestone to provide water for livestock. Some villages had three or four meres, which were clay lined. A few of these ancient meres still survive. For the naturalist, it is moorland ponds (**Above, Top**) that hold the most interest. Those fringed with cotton-grass, rushes and floating rafts of *Sphagnum* moss support the greatest diversity of species. **Bottom.** *Heathcote Mere near Hartington (SK 143 601) has been operative since (at least) 1482 and is now an important White Peak wildlife habitat.*

Book Information

To complement this book, O/S *Explorer* maps Nos. 0L1 and OL24 are required for map and compass work and general map reading. No walks overlap maps, so you only ever need one map. Better still, photocopy or scan and print the relevant area together with the route directions, and back to back them in a plastic A4 envelope. Use highlighter/pen to transcribe route/features from sketch maps to the O/S section. Most sketch maps contain information not on the O/S maps. Weatherproof the top with sticky tape, fold it up and put it in your pocket! Software such as *TrackLogs Digital Mapping* can enable the printing of larger scales. On wild walks, include sufficient area for an escape route. All the sketch maps and route descriptions in the book are presented on adjacent pages for ease of viewing. Words in **bold** in the route descriptions refer to features on the sketch maps and to many reference points on the ground. Likewise, many of the photos also serve this purpose. For uniformity, spelling throughout the book follows the O/S maps. The walks are described from north to south throughout The Peak. This does mean that some of the harder walks appear first, but it is the logical way to list them. As both *The Dark Peak* and *The White Peak* maps each have a west and east sheet, there are, in effect, four sections to the book - see page 8 for **Location of Walks**.

Map Reading / Times and Grades

Grid references are used throughout this book. It is taken for granted that the reader is familiar with them. If not, there is information on the O/S maps. Similarly, **compass bearings** are mentioned. There are many booklets and courses (or perhaps a friend) to explain map and compass work. What they may not mention is that much of your own paraphernalia can affect the compass : cameras, mobile phones, watches, ice axes and even wired bras to mention but a few, and overhead wires are serial culprits. Once learnt, map and compass skills are an invaluable aid to walking in mist and across open country. **Times and grades** are not given as they are too subjective. Most walkers average about 3 kms (1.88 miles) per hour during a walk. Add some time on for breaks. Determine your own capabilities on the shorter walks first. An early start should ensure a car space at the most popular venues. Public transport times/routes constantly change and are not listed.

Equipment

Footwear and **Clothing** are personal choices. Choose whatever you can afford and feel most comfortable in. I have never seen the logic in paying through the teeth to walk round advertising over-hyped brands. **Binoculars** (or a monocular) can be an invaluable aid in finding that stile at the end of a long field! **Trekking Poles** take the strain off ancient knees and can prevent falls when crossing streams or descending slippery paths. But remove or don't use the hand loops as, if you fall, you may not be able to arrest the fall with your hands; and always stow them before a scramble. **Mobile Phones** could raise help in an emergency - but should you fall in a gully on, say, Kinder, there will almost certainly be no signal. **Petroleum Jelly** (*Vaseline* etc) can prevent blisters if you're prone to them. Yucky, but it works. **GPS** (Global Positioning System) can locate your position to a few metres. An orange **Survival Bag** provides protection and can be seen from afar by rescue teams.

A survival bag is lightweight and inexpensive

Key To Sketch Maps

━━━━━	A roads
⟍⟍⟋	B roads, minor and unclassified roads
∿∿	River, canal or stream
⬭	Reservoir, lake or pond
───	Railway line
═══	Tram line
‣ – – – – ‣	Public footpath, bridleway or track marked on O/S map
▪ ▬ ▬ ▬ ▪	Concession or other path/track or route across open country not necessarily marked on O/S map

🏛 Stately home

✳ Point of interest

▲ Youth hostel

+ Aircraft wreck

✟ War memorial

Pennine Way Named path

🅿 Car park/start and finish of walk

▲ *Triangulation (trig) pillar, toposcope or other summit feature*

→ *Route direction*   260° → *Compass bearing across open country or access land*

Note *The representation on the maps of any path, track or road or route across open country and access land is no evidence of the existence of a right of way. Stiles have a habit of becoming gates etc and the walker should be aware of this in the **Route** data.*

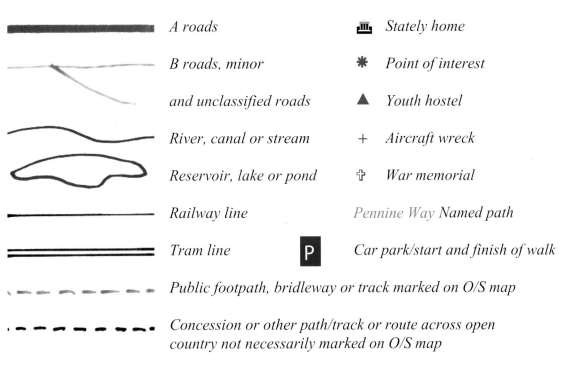

The maps in this book are all to scale and the routes can easily be transcribed onto the two required O/S maps using a highlighter pen. Maps published after the CRoW Act (19/09/04) show new areas of The Peak now accessible.

Waymark Colour Codes

⬆ Concession path

⬆ Public footpath

⬆ Public bridleway

The access land symbol together with public footpath waymark sign.

Walks On Dark Peak Map ——————— West Sheet

(Explorer Outdoor Leisure Series No 01)

Approaching Pym Chair on Kinder Scout (Walk 10, June 29). Pym Chair is one of many name duplications in The Peak (another Pym Chair is met on Walk 25). Other popular names include Deep Dale; the paradoxical High Low and Round Hill. Possibly the most frequent name in the Dark Peak is Featherbed Moss, which conjures up images of delightful walking terrain in the mind but in reality is nearly always an expanse of bog!

01 Wessenden Moor, Black Moss Reservoir and Shiny Brook Clough

On the track above Wessenden Reservoir (April 22). **Inset.** *Lichens beside the track.*

Our journey south through the Peak District starts with a trek across wild Wessenden Moor to Black Moss and Swellands Reservoirs. A paved section of The Pennine Way then leads to Wessenden Brook, which is followed to a picturesque waterfall. A track beside Wessenden Reservoir winds its way sedately uphill to Wessenden Head Reservoir where a footpath across the headwall leads to an off-path excursion up quiet Shiny Brook Clough.

Length 12 kms / 7.5 miles **Map** O/S Explorer OL1, *Dark Peak Area*, West Sheet
Start/Finish Lay-by on the north side of the A635 between Holmfirth and Greenfield at SE 050 063. Just west are two road signs. Depending which way you approach, you will see either *Oldham Metropolitan Borough, Saddleworth* or, *Kirklees in West Yorkshire*.
Terrain Wild in places, but not too strenuous a walk on a mixture of open peaty moorland with groughs; stony tracks and sections paved with Yorkshire flagstones.
Refreshments None on route. 3 kms E of the lay-by *The Ford* and *Huntsman* inns await.
When To Go/What's There The unpaved parts of Wessenden Moor can be a soggy trip after rain, so best to go after a few dry days. However, the waterfall that cascades through a bouquet of rhododendrons (in flower early June) soon dries up, so take your choice. The walk is mainly through moor grasses, but there are small stands of heather, bilberry, crowberry, cross-leaved heath and hare's-tail cotton-grass. Pools near Black Moss Reservoir support whirligig beetles, pond skaters, water crickets and common hawker and black darter dragonflies. April brings the return of the song of the curlew, skylark and willow warbler. There's the occasional raven, kestrel, snipe and golden plover and the odd dipper performs at Wessenden Brook. A few mountain hares roam the moor. Other flowers include coltsfoot, heath bedstraw, tormentil and foxglove.
Nearby Holmfirth has all you need if you're a fan of *Last Of The Summer Wine* (p.241).

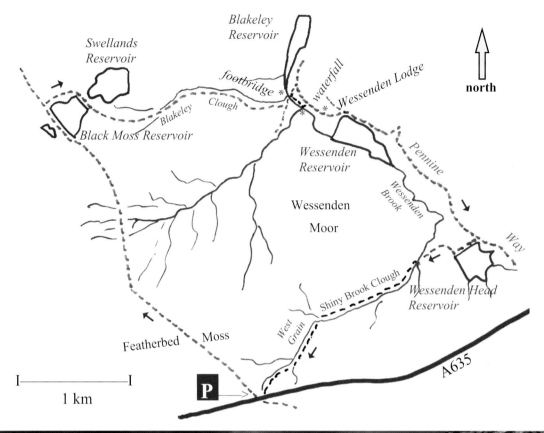

The footbridge across Wessenden Brook (Feb 15). **Inset.** *Hare's-tail cottongrass (June7)*

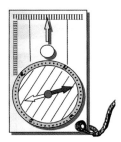

Route Go over the stile in the lay-by and take the path across the moor. The path soon becomes paved through the boggier regions. The paving peters out at steps to a grough. Posts then lead onwards to a fence, where a gate leads to the wildest part of the moor. However, there are posts (sticks) and cairns, so if the visibility is OK, you can thread your way through the groughs and the peat. If misty, a bearing of 340° will eventually bring you to **Black Moss Reservoir**. Walk across the western headwall (where there are some interesting relics) and, once over, turn right after about 100 metres onto the **Pennine Way**. Follow the path as it runs between Black Moss and **Swellands** Reservoirs. There is an awkward step over the outflow of Black Moss Reservoir, but this immediately leads to another paved section which wanders pleasantly across and then down the moor. After it ends, a path undulates down and up **Blakeley Clough** and, soon after, reaches a prominent, square concrete inspection shaft. Here, leave the main path and turn left, steeply downhill to the **footbridge** over **Wessenden Brook**. Don't take the uphill path, instead, turn right over the footbridge and follow the left bank upstream until you are level with the waterfall in the rhododendrons. Now turn 90° left, steeply uphill for about 50 metres to meet a track. Turn right, and follow the path as it wends its way sedately uphill beside **Wessenden Reservoir** to arrive at **Wessenden Head Reservoir**. Here, turn right and follow the path over the headwall which becomes a track as it swings right then left and ends at boulders. Manoeuvre carefully through the rocks, which soon end at a watercourse junction. Take the right fork and, after a few crossings, rise a little above the right bank and proceed above **Shiny Brook** until it veers to the left. Although this is still the major watercourse, it is now called **West Grain**. Here, descend to the brook and the way ahead is now more favourable on the left bank, which is followed until you can see traffic to the left on the **A635**. Shortly after, the watercourse becomes indiscernible, so ascend left, to the lay-by.

The welcome paving through the bog at the start of the walk is seemingly ignored by diehard "bog-trotters"! (April 22).

Above. *On the western headwall of Black Moss Reservoir (Sept 27). As well as a few flow relics, the reservoir also has two narrow sandy "beaches". Left of the headwall is Little Black Moss Reservoir which has aquatic wildlife.*

Left. *The waterfall which flows into Wessenden Brook is one of the most picturesque in the Peak District, but sadly frequently dries up (April 22).*

Below. *There is a small herd of deer in the grounds of Wessenden Lodge which is visible on the walk (April 22).*

02 Greenfield Reservoirs, Dovestone Rocks and Birchen Clough

Dovestone Reservoir and Alderman's Brow (right) from Ashway Rocks (Aug 24)

As you drive down the A635 from the east, and view the Greenfield reservoirs and edges for the first time, the impact is awesome and, for the walker, an irresistible outing. It starts with a steep pull up to Wimberry Stones from The Sugar Lump; follows Chew Green to Chew Hurdles and Chew Reservoir; links the viewpoints of Dish Stone Brow, Great Dovestone Rocks and Ashway Rocks; descends the falls in Birchen Clough and ends with a level stroll beside Greenfield, Yeoman Hey and Dovestone Reservoirs.

Length 14 kms / 8.75 miles **Map** O/S Explorer OL1, *Dark Peak Area*, West Sheet
Start/Finish Dovestone Reservoir Car Park off the A635 at SE 013 036. Conveniences.
Terrain A tough walk up and over rough ground on moorland paths, plus easy, level tracks. Map/compass skills essential in mist. Birchen Clough has to be taken with care.
Refreshments Weekend and summer snack bar at the car park
When To Go/What's There On a summer Sunday, the yachts on Dovestone Reservoir enhance the views, but this is tourist time, too. Boulderers perform on *The Sugar Lump* and the prongs of *The Trinnacle* at Raven Stones are merrily jumped upon. *Bramley's Cot* is a relict dwelling, but a poignant reminder of our mortality is the plaque on the cairn at Fox Stone. In 1968, Al Smith and myself nearly perished on the same Dolomite descent that claimed Tom Morton and Brian Toase in 1972. There is a memorial cross to MP James Platt who accidentally shot himself in 1857 (it never caught on). The King of Tonga (!) laid a stone at Yeoman Hey Reservoir in 1981. In summer, brown hawker and common darter dragonflies flutter above the plant-rich drains. Peregrine falcon and kestrel dominate the skies. There is little wreckage left of the Dakota which crashed on Wimberry Stones in 1949, killing 21 passengers and all 3 crew. 8 passengers survived one of the Dark Peak's worst air disasters. **Nearby** Alderman's Brow provides a spectacular view. The easy way up starts opposite Upperwood House (see sketch map).

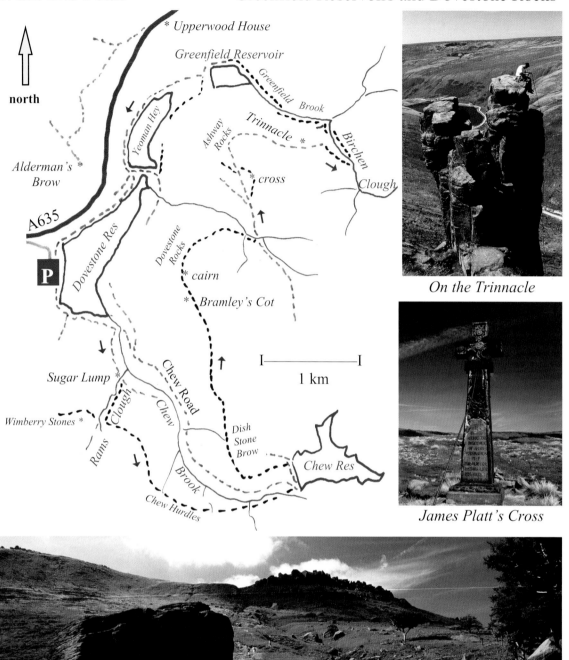

On the Trinnacle

James Platt's Cross

On the path from the Sugar Lump up to Wimberry Stones (Aug 3)

Route Walk past the sailing clubhouse on the left, go through a gate and soon turn right, off the track, at a wall entrance just before the track crosses a stream. Head up to a narrow path that runs below pine trees and above **Chew Brook**. The path leads to the square monolith of the **Sugar Lump** (nearby boulders have interesting graffiti). Turn right on the path which runs steeply up beside **Rams Clough**, to breach the edge just left of the **Wimberry Stones**. Once on top, turn left on the path which meanders to **Chew Reservoir**. Walk to the headwall and turn left, along the headwall path. As it veers right, leave the path and descend left onto an indistinct path across the moor, which at first runs parallel with **Chew Road**. The path soon leads to the edge proper and the viewpoint rocks of **Dish Stone Brow**. Onwards, the path may be faint in places so keep close to the edge to pick it up again and, after about 2 kms, to reach the ruin of **Bramley's Cot**, visible in rocks just below the main path. Soon after, the **cairn** appears and then the viewpoint at **Dove Stone Rocks**. The path, now mainly over peat, contours round a watercourse. Shortly after, take the right fork to reach the memorial **cross**. From here, descend a little to pick up the main path which swings right and runs above the conspicuous **Ashway Rocks**, being careful not to take any paths down to the valley. Soon the popular **Trinnacle** appears at Raven Stones. Continue past it for about 300m, until you are able to leave the path and descend left to a stream in **Birchen Clough**. Cross where you can and turn left. Follow the narrow, undulating path, fragile in places, beside the stream (or a higher, more sound one), passing some fine falls on the way (see below) to the bottom of the clough. Here, cross the stream where you feel fit, turn right and head to a metal footbridge over a watercourse which disappears into a tunnel to the left. Cross the bridge and pick up a track which at first runs to the left of **Greenfield Brook**, before crossing to the right. The track hugs the right bank of **Greenfield Reservoir**. By following the obvious paths nearest the right (west) banks of **Yeoman Hay** and **Dovestone Reservoirs**, you arrive back at the car park.

A delightful spot to rest near the bottom of Birchen Clough (Aug 3) See also p.27.

Above. *Looking down on the yacht races on Dovestone Reservoir from Dish Stone Brow.*
Below. *Alderman's Hill from the path to the Sugar Lump (both Aug 3).*

03 Crowden Little Brook, Meadow Clough and Laddow Castles

Entering the bivouac at one of Laddow Castles (March 6)

The conventional route to Black Hill from Crowden is to ascend Westend Moss and return via Laddow Rocks on The Pennine Way. This route is sometimes called the Crowden Horseshoe, but does not visit the lovely series of waterfalls of Crowden Little Brook nor the spectacular sight of Crowden Great Brook plunging through a ravine beneath Laddow Castles. The castles are a group of weathered craggy outcrops and dominate one of the wildest scenes in the Peak District. This short but tough walk has the added interest of visiting the wreckage of two Meteor jets which crashed in 1951.

Length 10 kms / 6.25 miles **Map** O/S Explorer OL1, *Dark Peak Area*, West Sheet
Start/Finish Crowden car park (with conveniences) off the A628 at SK 072 993.
Terrain A tough hill walk, half of which is off paths and on rough ground. Map and compass skills required. There is a near vertical drop into Crowden Great Brook from the highest Laddow Castle, but here is the view! There is a very steep descent to the valley after the Castles, where trekking poles would be beneficial. A wild walk to remember.
Refreshments Campsite shop near CP. Crowden Youth Hostel serves meals, but book.
When To Go/What's There This is not a walk for icy, snowy or misty conditions. There is a bivouac at one of the castles (photo above). Wildlife includes mountain hare, peregrine falcon, kestrel, ring ouzel, dipper, golden plover and raven. Some of the pools and bogs support dragonflies, pond skaters, water-crowfoot, marsh pennywort and heath spotted-orchid. Green hairstreak butterflies fly in spring and cuddly fox moth caterpillars abound late summer. Scattered wreckage of the two Meteors which crashed at the head of Meadow Clough killing both pilots, is easy to find. The largest remnant lies at SE 06861 02860 (GPS reading, photo p.48). The end of the walk passes Brockholes Wood Nature Reserve (info board). **Nearby** Black Hill summit disappoints, so try Digley and Bilberry Reservoirs to Nether Lane and return via waterfalls of Dean Clough. (P at SE 110 072).

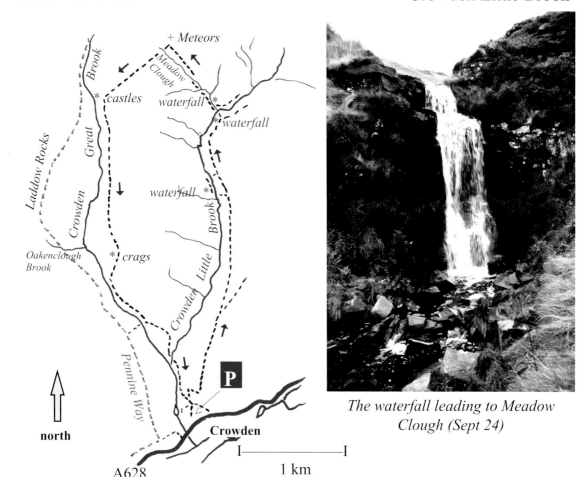

The waterfall leading to Meadow Clough (Sept 24)

On the track to the first waterfall (April 29). **Inset.** *A Meteor's impact pool.*

Route Turn right at the toilets and walk ahead at the track junction. After a few metres, turn right off the track, go over a stile and walk up the stony path which leads steeply uphill to another stile and an access land sign. Over the stile the path widens to a track and the angle eases. Soon **Crowden Little Brook** comes into view down to the left. After about 1½ kms, a couple of trees can be seen at the brook. Just after them, descend from the track to the first **waterfall**. It is best to arrive above the fall by striding over the water a few metres upstream. Now walk up the rocky watercourse ahead until the slabs peter out and ascend right to the track again. Soon after, the track becomes a path and a second waterfall is seen below, and Holme Moss TV mast ahead. After an old stone sheepfold on the left, the path forks down to a prominent watercourse. About 50 metres up is a fine **waterfall**. Walk towards the waterfall and climb the steep, left bank before it. Above the fall, the watercourse splits into two smaller falls. Take the left bank of the left fall. At the top is a grouse butt on the right, but ahead (bearing 324°), can be seen the start of **Meadow Clough**. Walk up the left side until the clough forks and peters out. Here, ahead and to the right can be seen the remains of the **Meteors**. Tracks lead to various remains, but from the largest piece of wreckage (p.48), set your compass to 240° and walk about 1 km over the moor to arrive at **Laddow Castles**. Ascend the highest for the views and, as you look south, to your left (east) you will see the ridge you next have to attain, which is most easily done by descending left then angling up right. At the top, walk just below the bilberry banks until a miniscule path leads on. Pass **Laddow Rocks** across the valley and then the cleft of **Oakenclough Brook**. Soon after, start your descent. Angle left and keep left of some crags with a small pinnacle (good perch) at their left end, then descend steeply to the valley floor, to the path beside **Crowden Great Brook**. Turn left, pass storm damage to the path; ignore a metal footbridge and keep ahead to eventually reach another footbridge. Cross, turn right; pass Brockenholes Nature Reserve on your left en route to the car park.

High above Crowden Great Brook on the way to Laddow Castles (Aug 18)

Top Left. *There is an easy optional scramble at the first waterfall.* **Top Right.** *On the rocky stretch of Crowden Little Brook above the first waterfall (both Sept 24). The top of the fall is a magical place. Many years ago, the watercourse changed direction and the fall is now at 90° to the stream. The original watercourse can still be seen beside the fall.* **Above.** *Looking to Holme Moss TV mast from the largest piece of the Meteors' wreckage.*

Bleaklow Stones and Two Black Cloughs

Wreckage of the Botha on Bleaklow Meadows (Nov 10)

This short, tough but exhilarating day out starts beside the wide, rocky stream falling through Birchen Bank Wood. One of the most picturesque waterfalls in The Peak is passed up the wilds of Middle Black Clough en route to two aircraft wrecks. The natural rock sculptures at Bleaklow Stones are followed by a descent of scenic Far Black Clough.

Length 10 kms / 6.25 miles **Map** O/S Explorer OL1, *Dark Peak Area*, West Sheet
Start/Finish Parking area near bottom of slip road to Woodhead Tunnel, off the A628, 2 kms E of Woodhead Bridge at SK 114 998. There are also lay-bys above on the A628.
Terrain The way up Middle Black Clough has to be taken with care. It is rocky, uneven and in some places slippery and loose. Trekking poles would facilitate the fording (twice) of the wide stream in Birchen Bank Wood. There are pathless sections up and over moors and bogs where map/compass skills are required. But don't be deterred by all this!
Refreshments None on route. Mobile hot/cold snacks at the large lay-by on the A628.
When To Go/What's There Not recommended when there is snow or ice. When the heather is out, the cloughs are wild delights. Crowberry, cloudberry and cowberry also flourish. Kestrel, peregrine and dragonfly hunt; mountain hares are in abundance. Golden plover and grouse take to the air. The vivid, mossy banks of upper Far Black Clough are unusual. The streams have dipper, grey wagtail, water crickets and whirligig beetles. Wing wreckage of the Blackburn Botha, which crashed in Dec 1941 killing the pilot, is seen on Bleaklow Meadows. The wreckage cairn and remembrances to the two airmen who died at Near Bleaklow Stones, when their Boulton Paul Defiant came down in August 1941, is visited. The airmen survived the crash but sadly subsequently died from their injuries and exposure. A farmer found them seated by the fuselage a month later. Near *The Anvil* is a well-carved boulder (1850) atop of which is a fine panorama.
Nearby Spectacular Ramsden Clough may now be visited via access land (see p 242).

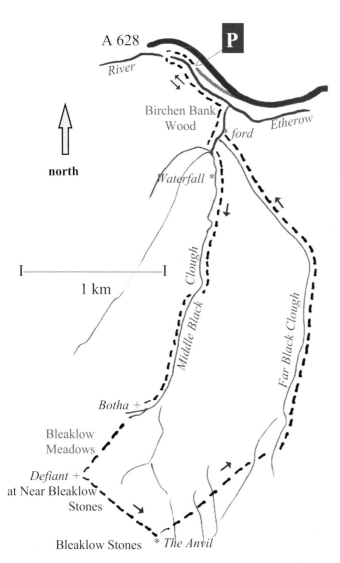

Golden plover's nest on Bleaklow Meadows (April 5)

Upper Middle Black Clough (Sept 4)

The waterfall in Middle Black Clough (Sept 4)

Route From the parking area, walk down to the bridge over the **River Etherow**. Before crossing the river, you may wish to have a look at the sealed entrances to the Woodhead Tunnel and the associated information board. Cross the river and turn left over a stile. Follow the right bank, climb another stile and the track leads to a **ford**. Don't cross, but follow the right bank of the wide stream until progress is barred at a low cascade. Cross the stream via the various permutations of boulders in the water. A path of sorts now starts to rise through the heather and rocks. Stay on the left bank of the stream as it forks, this will soon bring you to the major **waterfall** in **Middle Black Clough**. After another hour or more of hard going, a huge slab of rock in the stream is encountered. A couple of hundred metres after this, or where you think appropriate, cross the stream and climb up to the path which runs above the right bank of the stream. Progress is now quicker and the path eventually falls to the stream. About 150 metres after this, leave the stream and turn right up a watercourse. About 70 metres up, it forks into two peaty groughs. Take the right fork and, after about 15 metres, climb out of the grough on its right bank. Before you (bearing 340°) about 80 metres away, is the wreck of the **Botha**. From here, walk on a bearing of 220° over **Bleaklow Meadows** and up to **Near Bleaklow Stones**. Aim for the top of a lighter coloured grass gulley. Here is the wreck of the **Defiant**. From here, a bearing of 136° SE will bring you to **Bleaklow Stones**, which can be seen about 1 km away. From **The Anvil**, walk downhill on a bearing of 50° NE, crossing a number of groughs until you arrive in a deep watercourse, which is the start of **Far Black Clough**. A path soon appears on the right bank. After 2 kms, it becomes a track which leads back to the ford at the start of the walk. After heavy rain, the stream is best forded a few metres upstream.

The Anvil (sometimes called The Shoe Last) at Bleaklow Stones (Sept 4)

On the track above Far Black Clough (Sept 4). For those of you with GPS, the Botha lies at SK 110 974 (photo page 49) and most Defiant remains at SK 106 970.

05 Wildboar Clough, Sykes Moor and Torside Clough

Looking to Torside Reservoir from above the ancient wood (Aug 20)

Our second walk to the northern flanks of Bleaklow is of equal stature to Walk 4 and, should you so wish, provides one of the most challenging scrambles in The Peak. The route rises through an ancient oak and silver birch wood to the bottom of Wildboar Clough, where a choice of routes both lead to the top of the clough. Sykes Moor is then crossed to the wreckage of a Blenheim which crashed in January 1939. Torside Grain leads to a fine viewpoint of upper Torside Clough, then a descent to a level stroll back.

Length 8 kms / 5 miles **Map** O/S Explorer OL1, *Dark Peak Area*, West Sheet
Start/Finish Torside Car Park and PCs off the B6105 at SK 068 983
Terrain To ascend Wildboar Clough direct you will certainly need rock climbing skills, although the crux obstacles can all be avoided left or right. The ascent of White Mare into the clough is on steep, rough ground. Be prepared for rocky paths and off-path moors.
Refreshments Café occasionally open at the car park, most often on summer weekends.
When To Go/What's There Despite its cult reputation, Wildboar Clough has some lovely falls, pools and rocky stairs and, taken with care, is an exuberant ascent; but not recommended when ice/snow prevail. The pools support water-crickets and pond-skaters. A memorial to the two airmen who perished in the crash of the Blenheim L1476 is reached after a short crossing of lofty Sykes Moor, where mountain hare and goshawk roam. There is a delightful bilberry knoll at the bottom of Torside Grain, which hovers above the cascades of upper Torside Clough. The *Pennine Way* is descended to the *Trans Pennine Trail* beside which, in summer, meadow brown and small heath butterflies flit around harebell, hawkweed, trefoil, meadow vetchling and clover. Drains support bog pondweeds and whirligig beetles twirl. At weekends, the Glossop and District Sailing Club perform on Torside Reservoir. **Nearby** Now on access land, Cock Hill (SK 059 962) can be reached in a circular walk starting from near Moorside, Old Glossop.

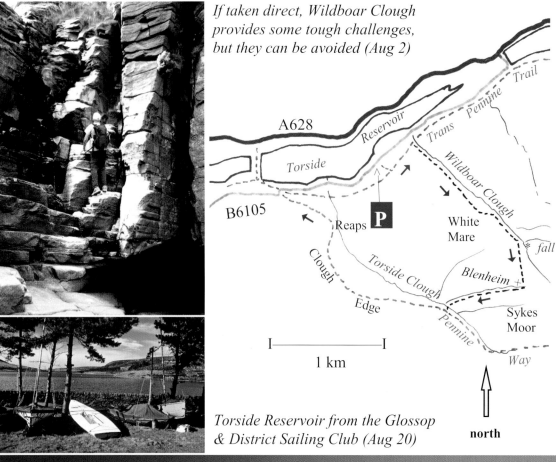

If taken direct, Wildboar Clough provides some tough challenges, but they can be avoided (Aug 2)

Torside Reservoir from the Glossop & District Sailing Club (Aug 20)

The memorial at the Blenheim crash site on Sykes Moor (SK 083 971, Feb 20)

Route Walk up to the top left corner of the car park, go through a gate and turn left on the **Trans Pennine Trail**. After about 200 metres, there is a signpost to Wildboar Clough, so turn right and ascend the few steps to the stile. The path leads to another wooden stile at a fence and onwards uphill through bracken to the relict woodland. In high summer, the path ahead may be almost obscured by bracken in places, but battle on to soon emerge from the wood onto a heather and grassy bank with fine views behind. The path through the heather ends at a fence/stile.

To ascend Wildboar Clough direct, walk ahead up a narrow path that later falls to the bottom rubble of the clough. However, to avoid the lower problems, highly recommended for a first visit is to turn right over the stile to another about 50m away. Over, turn left; walk up beside a wire fence to another fence. Turn right and, after about 60m, go over the access stile. Now slant left, to meet the uphill fence again. You are now on the exposed flanks of **White Mare**. Keep to the right of the fence until the incline relents at the start of a bilberry/peat bank. Soon after, an access stile allows you to cross the fence and turn right along a narrow path above **Wildboar Clough**. Follow the path and descend carefully into the clough at your convenience. Turn right, go up rocky slabs and then a fine rocky staircase

Looking into upper Torside Clough (Aug 20)

(photo) to more slabs. After another 400m, the final waterfall rocks in the clough appear, about 4m high, in 3-tiers. Above and to the right of the **fall** is a stile. Go over and walk south (176°) for about ½ km across **Sykes Moor** (which instils a wonderful feeling of freedom) to the memorial and wreckage at the site of the **Blenheim** crash, which lies partially obscured in a shallow gully (photo). Now walk half-right down shallow gullies until you can see a conspicuous, isolated knoll way below you. Head down to it. From the top there are fine views into **Torside Clough** (photo, left). Across the clough is the **Pennine Way**, so descend from the knoll, cross the stream and select a suitable (for you) steep ascent to the path. Turn right, and descend above crags and down **Clough Edge** to the dwellings at **Reaps**. The way now veers to the left and descends to the **B6105**, where a complex of gates grant access to the Trans Pennine Trail again. Turn right, and stroll 1½ kms back to the car park.

Wonderful walking up the rocky staircase in upper Wildboar Clough (Aug 20)

06 Lady Clough, Bleaklow, Grains in the Water and Alport Dale

Approaching the trig pillar at Higher Shelf Stones (June 7)

This tough but rewarding excursion to the Bleaklow plateau starts with an undulating walk up Lady Clough to the ancient way of Doctor's Gate; briefly joins the Pennine Way before ascending Higher Shelf Stones for two aircraft wrecks, then, off-path, crosses to the shattered rocks of Yellowslacks (blown-up by landowners to deter climbers!); visits the Kissing Stones and hidden waterfalls of Alport Dale and finally rises steeply beside Nether Reddale Clough to an off-path stretch and an aerial view of (hopefully), your car.

Length 13 kms / 8.13 miles **Map** O/S Explorer OL1, *Dark Peak Area*, West Sheet
Start/Finish Birchin Clough Bridge car park, on the A57 at SK 109 914
Terrain Well-defined paths together with some off-path peat bogs and moorland forays and so map/compass skills essential in case of bad weather. There is a gentle rise to Higher Shelf Stones, but the sting in the tail is the steep climb out of Alport Dale.
Refreshments None on route but there is an occasional mobile café at the car park and the **Nearby** *Snake Inn* is usually open all day.
When To Go/What's There Go after a few dry days when the peat sections will be easier. In autumn and early winter the grasses and rushes turn red and gold and in winter the coat of the mountain hare is white, making it easy for us (and predators) to see when there is no snow. Plants include cloudberry, cotton-grass, goldenrod and bog asphodel; butterwort and hard shield-fern flourish at some waterfalls in Alport Dale. Several *Sphagnum* bogs provide a splash of vivid green amongst the peat. Peregrine falcon, snipe, kestrel, common lizard, voles and dragonflies may appear. Rove, tiger and burying beetles often cross the paths and oil beetles frequent boggy flushes. Wreckage of the Superfortress RB-29A (*Over Exposed*) which crashed in November 1948 killing all 13 crew, lies near Higher Shelf Stones and the remains of the Lancaster KB993, which flew into James's Thorn in May 1945 killing all 6 crew, are beneath Lower Shelf Stones.

Engine remains of the Superfortress "Over Exposed" (Aug 19)

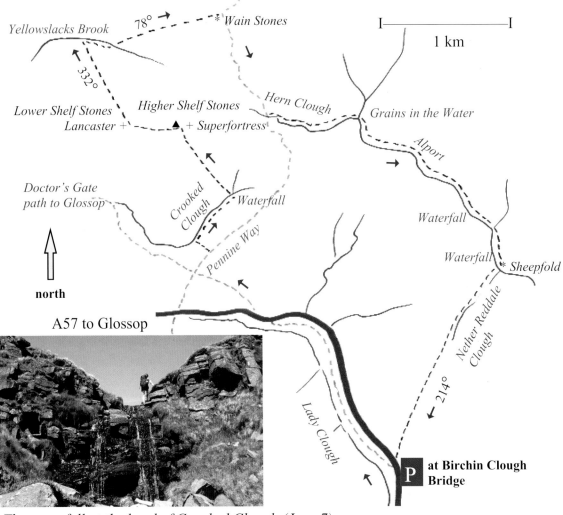

The waterfall at the head of Crooked Clough (June 7)

Route Take the entrance to **Lady Clough** opposite the car park and walk upstream on the undulating path until a second culvert is reached. Shortly after, the path peters out at the **A57** which is walked up for 200 metres (narrow path on left) until, on the opposite side, the signposted **Doctor's Gate** is reached. Follow this path across the moor until the **Pennine Way** (PW) is reached at a signpost. Turn right on the PW and, immediately after the only flight of steps, bear left down a watercourse until the narrow path which runs above and parallel to **Crooked Clough** is reached. Turn right and follow the path upstream until a **waterfall** is reached at the head of the clough. Walk past the fall, and the path now runs left, uphill, (occasionally indistinct) to the engraved rocks and trig point at **Higher Shelf Stones**. Set your compass to 70° and walk east for about a minute to the Superfortress wreck. Return to the trig pillar, and follow the edge down to the crags of **Lower Shelf Stones**. Continue downhill on the path for about 250 metres until the Lancaster wreckage is reached (if you have GPS the reference is 0805 9473). Now set compass to **332°** and walk across wild terrain to the shattered, rocky gash of **Yellowslacks Brook**. Walk up the stream to a unique semi-circular rock terrace (lunch?). Here, leave the brook on a bearing of **78°** and walk gently uphill to the **Wain Stones** then continue on for about 100 metres to meet the PW again. Turn right and follow the track for about 1 km to a ford with 5 stepping stones. Here, a path leaves the PW and follows the left bank of the stream downhill. This is **Hern Clough**, and leads to **Grains in the Water** and **Alport Dale**, passing waterfalls until remains of a square **sheepfold** appear below. Descend to the fold and turn right upstream to a hidden **waterfall** (photo). Return to the fold, cross the river and ascend the steep, right rim of the clough (**Nether Reddale**). At the top, follow a bearing of **214°** across the moor, to meet a path which descends steeply to the car park.

*Near to this waterfall in Alport Dale, hundreds of common butterwort plants (**Inset**) grow on a damp wall of shale (both July 20). They usually flower in mid June.*

The Wain Stones are often called The Kissing Stones as, from a number of angles, they resemble a couple about to kiss. Legendary Alfred Wainwright documented such.

At the atmospheric Grains in the Water (Nov 22)

07 Fair Brook, Gun Rock, Kinder Edge and Ashop Clough

Ascending the dry, summit waterfalls of Fair Brook. **Inset.** *Cloudberry (both July 21).*

This is the first of our four routes up Kinder Scout and arguably the most scenic ascent, especially when the heather is flowering (see photo p.13). It follows the right bank of Fair Brook to the summit waterfalls, from which there is an optional detour to Gun Rock. From Fairbrook Naze, Kinder Edge is followed west and, shortly after the weathered rocks of The Boxing Gloves, the route descends to Black Ashop Moor to visit wreckage of two Sabre jets that collided in mid-air. Ashop Clough is then followed downstream to a footbridge, over which a path rises to Rough Bank and Nungrain and back to the start.

Length 12 kms / 7.5 miles **Map** O/S Explorer OL 1, *Dark Peak Area*, West Sheet
Start/Finish A few small lay-bys just SE of the *Snake Inn* on the A57 at SK 113 904
Terrain Mostly on sandy and stony paths, but there is rough open ground to the aircraft wreck. The final pull up to Kinder Edge is steep. There may be boggy places after rain.
Refreshments None on route, but the *Snake Inn* near the lay-bys is usually open all day.
When To Go/What's There As with other routes to the Kinder plateau, there are the usual blanket-bog suspects including mountain hare, meadow pipit, red grouse and golden plover. Bracken is gradually ousting the heather from Fair Brook but action is at last being taken as experimental spraying with the herbicide *Asulox* has begun. *Hygrocybe miniata*, a small red toadstool that has no common name, may be seen beside the path up in late summer/autumn. Green tiger beetles, lizards and emperor moth larvae may also cross the path. Water-crickets skate over pools. Bilberry, cloudberry, heather, crowberry and cross-leaved heath are wildlife food-plants. Kestrels and dragonflies hawk above. Butterflies include green hairstreak in April/May and small heath in summer. Wreckage of the two Sabre F86 jets which collided above Black Ashop Moor in July 1954, killing both pilots, lies at SK 075 902. **Nearby** on Edale Moor at SK 101 878, lie engine remains of an Avro Anson which crashed in Dec 1944. All on board survived.

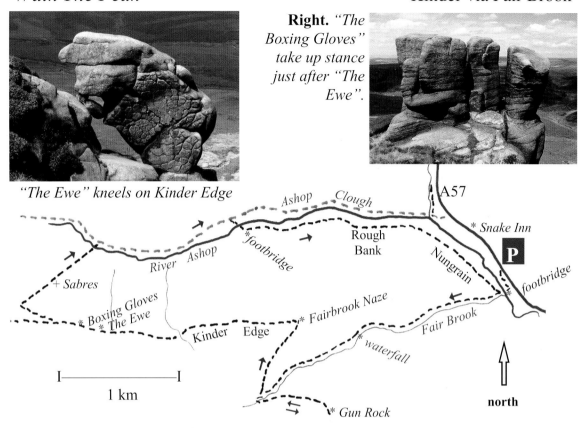

Right. *"The Boxing Gloves" take up stance just after "The Ewe".*

"The Ewe" kneels on Kinder Edge

Gun Rock should perhaps be renamed Posers' Rock! (Dec 28)

Route Between the lower two lay-bys, and on the opposite side of the road, is a stile. Over it, the path runs parallel to the **A57** before swinging to the right through the wood to a **footbridge** over the **River Ashop**, where there is a wonderful, ancient rowan tree. Cross the river, turn left and the path bends to the right to arrive at the bottom of **Fair Brook**. The path on the right bank is followed all the way upstream to the start of the huge boulders near the summit, and on to where the terraced waterfall rocks begin. Here, it is possible to walk and scramble up to the top if they are reasonably dry. If not, follow the steep path on the right . If you wish to visit **Gun Rock**, turn left at the top and follow the path along the edge for about ½ km to the rock (photo). Return to the top of Fair Brook and now follow the path north to the weathered tors of **Fairbrook Naze**. From here, the path swings west to run along **Kinder Edge** for about 2 kms before **The Ewe** appears on the right (photo). 100 metres on are **The Boxing Gloves** (photo). About 150 metres on from the famous outcrop, the path forks. At this point, on a bearing of 330°, wreckage of the **Sabres** can be seen on the moor below. Either walk steeply down to the remains, or take the lower path for about another ½ km and turn right down a less steep incline to them. A faint path leads from the crash site across the moor (one grough to negotiate) to the fledgling River Ashop and, a few metres above, to the path which runs the length of **Ashop Clough**. Turn right and follow the path downstream to the footbridge across the river, which is near a ruin. Cross the footbridge and turn left up the path, being careful not to take the track uphill at low, wooden fencing. The path undulates high above Ashop Clough, with fine views ahead and behind, traverses **Rough Bank**, rounds Urchin Clough and crosses marshy **Nungrain** before dropping down to the **footbridge** at the start of the walk.

Rounding Urchin Clough on the way to Nungrain (Aug 11). I was bitten by an adder whilst kneeling in the heather to take the above photo, so keep to the path!

Crossing the River Ashop onto Rough Bank (Aug 23)

Wing wreckage of the Sabres. **Inset.** *More remains lie above (both Aug 11). The Boxing Gloves can just be seen at the right end of the Kinder Edge skyline.*

08 Kinder Reservoir, The Mermaid's Pool and Hollingworth Clough

On the path beside Kinder Reservoir (Dec 27)

This adventurous hike starts from where the mass trespassers over Kinder Scout set out in 1932. A plaque at the CP commemorates their heroics, without which, access to open country may not have been granted for decades. Kinder Reservoir is followed to the Mermaid's Pool. A steep pull up to the crags of Sandy Heys earns easier walking to Mill Hill and the wreckage of the Liberator B-24J which crashed on October 11,1944. From an enchanting waterfall in Hollingworth Clough, the route rises to The Knott then falls to two white cabins and finally a fabulous aerial view of Kinder Scout and its reservoir.

Length 12 kms / 7.5 miles **Map** O/S Explorer OL 1, *Dark Peak Area*, West Sheet
Start/Finish Bowden Bridge CP (take Kinder Road from Hayfield) at SK 048 869
Terrain A tough slog over diverse terrain: ranging from well-defined paths over moors and open ground, to rough, steep heath, up and over trackless access land. Start early.
Refreshments None on route, but you pass through Hayfield on your drive home.
When To Go/What's There Kinder Reservoir sees the ubiquitous Canada goose plus sporadic visitors including heron, cormorant, lesser black-backed gull and goosander. Grey wagtail, dipper and common sandpiper visit the River Kinder but the richest assemblage of wildlife is found at the Mermaid's Pool, where dragonflies, damselflies, water beetles, frogs, cotton-grass and rushes flourish. Other birds include raven, kestrel and wren. Approaching Sandy Heys we once saw five mountain hares and four lizards on one trip. The rocks beneath have odd graffiti. Cross-leaved heath, ling and bell heather bloom in lower Hollingworth Clough which then resembles a glen. The Liberator crew survived the crash, and undercarriage, wing and engine remains can be seen. For those of you with GPS, the largest amount of wreckage lies at SK 05853 90637, with the wing wreckage 100 metres NW in shallow gullies close to the paved path. **Nearby** The Sett Valley Trail starts from Hayfield, and can be used to gain footpaths up Lantern Pike.

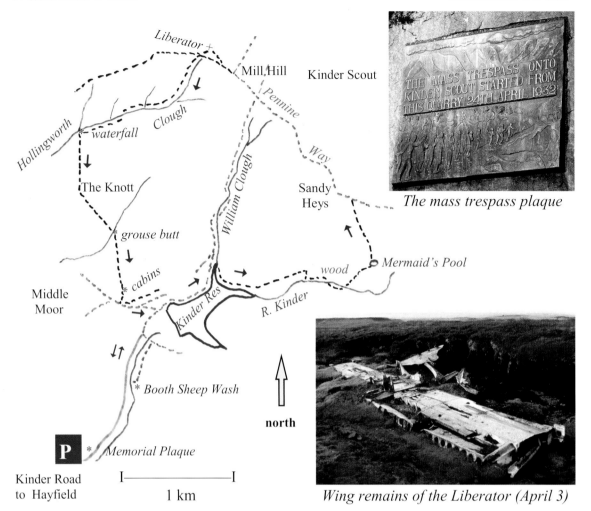

The mass trespass plaque

Wing remains of the Liberator (April 3)

Looking to Mill Hill and upper Hollingworth Clough from above the waterfall (Sept 4)

Route Turn left out of the CP and follow the lane to Booth **sheep wash** (info board). Go ahead through the gates to more gates. To the left is an inlaid path (NT sign *White Brow*). Head up the path and continue beside the reservoir until the stream tumbling down **William Clough** is reached. Cross the stream and turn right. This path soon leaves the reservoir and rises to cross fields and flushes to reach a larch **wood**. Here, turn right and descend to the **River Kinder**. Bear left, upstream. Depending on conditions, the river may have to be crossed a few times.

Level with the end of the wood are a number of waterfalls. Ensure you are on the left bank before the falls to enable you to slant up through the wood to the top right corner. Here, go over/through the wall/fence and slant 45° right, uphill, until the **Mermaid's Pool** appears on level ground after about 100m. Above the western end of the pool a wall can be seen (photo p.68) rising to the crags of **Sandy Heys**. Select your own line up to the crags, which are easily breached. Above the crags you meet the **Pennine Way**. Turn left on the well-worn path to the end of the edge, where it descends as a stone staircase. At the bottom, keep right at the fork to a post with four named destinations. (Here, if you're short of time or energy, turn left down William Clough back to the reservoir). Go ahead at the post and up to the "summit" of **Mill Hill**, where there is a wooden stake. Here, the *Pennine Way* turns right, but walk ahead and descend on flagstones for about 300m until, at a 90° left turn, a narrow path leads ahead (310°) to undercarriage, fuselage and engine remains of the **Liberator**, ever sinking into the peat. Now, angle just left (260°) back towards the pavé, where wing and more remains lie in a shallow gulley, very close to the path. Turn left, cross the paving to a faint path that leads (230°) through the heather. Ahead, the mound of **The Knott** is

Bell heather at the waterfall in scenic Hollingworth Clough (July 17)

prominent. Walk towards it and angle down left to the main watercourse which is the start of **Hollingworth Clough**. Keep to the right bank where you will find (and quickly lose) vestigial paths. After about 1km the terrain diverts you to the left bank and soon leads to above the **waterfall**, found where a prominent gulley falls into the clough from the right (steep drop here, care; optional descent to the fall further left). From above the fall, struggle south (180°) up to The Knott, using the mossier ground to facilitate a zigzag to the summit. From the top, at 170°, two white cabins can be seen, with a distinct path leading to them. Head downhill (130°) to meet this path at a grouse butt and turn right to the **cabins**. Here, bear right for 50m to another path, turn left and then right at the fork 30m on (post, *bridleway*). The path descends and swings left. Just before a green FP sign, turn right, steeply down to the start of the reservoir.

First views of Kinder Scout from the reservoir (Dec 27)

Tadpole observation at the Mermaid's Pool, with Sandy Heys above (April 3).

09 Kinder via Blackden Brook, Upper Tor and Madwoman's Stones

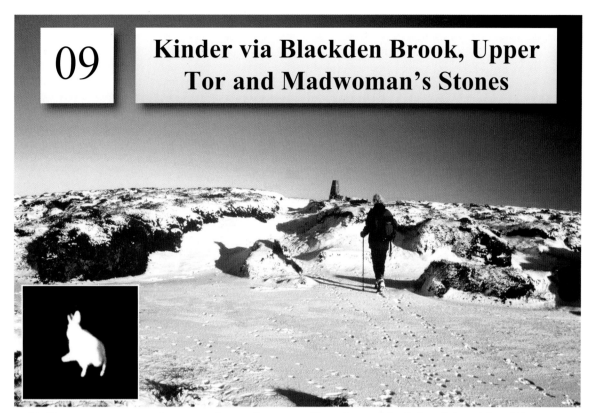

Following mountain hare tracks to the trig pillar above Blackden Edge (Nov 29). **Inset.**
An apparition in flight is all the walker usually glimpses of the mountain or blue hare in winter, especially when there is no snow to camouflage its seasonal colour change.

This short but serious adventure ascends Kinder Scout by its wildest northern route; crosses the plateau at its narrowest point for views from Kinder's southern crags; visits aircraft remains above Blackden Edge and memorably plummets back down Dean Hill.

Length 8 kms / 5 miles **Map** O/S Explorer OL 1, *Dark Peak Area*, on E and W Sheet
Start/Finish A rutty lay-by beside the A57 at SK 131 895, 2 km SE of *Snake Inn*
Refreshments None on route. *Snake Inn, Ladybower Inn* and lay-by mobiles are nearby
Terrain Most of the walk is off recognised paths. Rocky Blackden Brook has to be crossed a number of times, and there are several places, especially above the highest waterfall, where extreme caution has to be exercised at loose, steep, rocky and slippery situations. Once up, map and compass skills required. However, taken with care, this is a wonderful venture up, across and down Kinder Scout. Not fun in places after heavy rain.
When To Go/What's There If you go in snow/ice, ensure you are experienced in winter mountaineering. However, after snow, the tracks of mountain hares, stoats and voles criss-cross the route. The occasional dipper and heron may be spotted at the start of the walk, and butterwort and water-crowfoot flower in flushes beside Blackden Brook. Wrens, thought of as urban birds, flit up the cloughs, as do migrant waders in winter. Kestrel and peregrine falcon hawk above, while golden plover, meadow pipit and red grouse risk the plateau, which is composed of crowberry, bilberry and moor grasses. Cloudberry and cross-leaved heath may be found. Remnants of the Halifax HR727 which crashed in Oct 1943 killing five crew are visited near the trig pillar above Blackden Edge (GPS 131 876). **Nearby** a Wellington crash site at Upper Tor has been plundered.

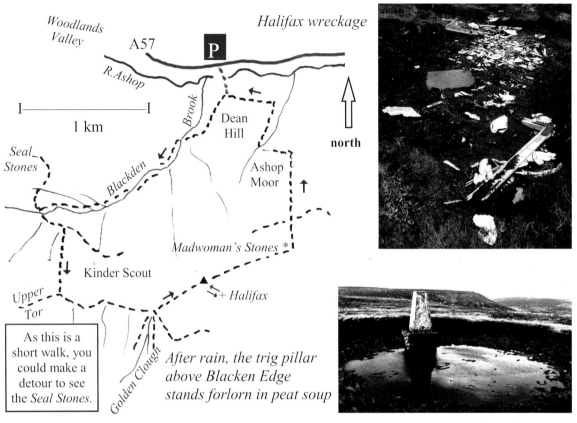

Woodlands Valley

A57

P

R.Ashop

Halifax wreckage

I————————I
1 km

Brook

Dean Hill

north

Seal Stones

Blackden

Ashop Moor

Madwoman's Stones *

Kinder Scout

+ Halifax

Upper Tor

As this is a short walk, you could make a detour to see the *Seal Stones.*

Golden Clough

After rain, the trig pillar above Blacken Edge stands forlorn in peat soup

The footbridge over the R. Ashop was almost swept away in the flash floods of Aug 2002

Route Go through the gate in the lay-by, walk down the path and cross the **River Ashop** by the footbridge. The path then rises to a wall. Go through another gate and take the path across the moor above **Blackden Brook** and Blackden Barns. The path eventually descends to the brook. Find an appropriate place to cross the brook. The path now largely runs up the right bank but, higher up, the brook has to be re-crossed a number of times. There is a stile to cross, too. The final, steep ascent to the summit rocks is performed on the right bank. Turn left at the top and walk 100 metres or so to a prominent watercourse coming in from the right. Take the path ahead (not the path left along the edge) to another watercourse about 50 metres ahead. Cross it and immediately leave the main path for a narrow path on the right. This leads in 15-20 minutes to the southern edge of Kinder, near to **Upper Tor**. Turn left on the track (some paved) for about ¾ km until it leads downhill to meet a path (with ludicrous cairn) joining from the right (from **Golden Clough**). Here, turn left up a peaty path and go on a bearing of 64° for a long 300 metres to the trig pillar. (Depending on the viscosity of the peat, you could also follow the "path" as it groughs its way there). To find the **Halifax** wreckage, walk on a bearing of 130° from the trig pillar, for about 250 metres, to the site. Retrace your steps (310°) to the pillar and take the path (of sorts) which leads (70°) past a couple of eroded outcrops to the **Madwoman's Stones** proper. Here, turn left and head north (360°) down the moor, crossing paths and taking sheep trails to a very steep slope high above **Ashop Moor**. Far below is a wall which runs from left to right across the moor. Thread your way down to the wall, taking the least steep lines. Turn left at the wall until it meets the head of a clough. At this point the wall veers left and, far below you if the visibility is OK, Hayridge Farm off the **A57** and the track to Alport Farm is framed in the V of the clough. Cross to the left bank and walk down the shoulder of the clough, which is on **Dean Hill**. As you descend, there are unparalleled views of the **Woodlands Valley**. Way below is another wall. Before the bottom of the shoulder, faint trails lead down left to the wall. Turn left on the narrow path beside the wall which returns you to the gate above Blackden Barns, near to the start of the walk.

Winter wanderings near Upper Tor, Kinder Scout after early snow (Nov 29)

Left. *Blackden Brook from about half way up.*
Right. *Nearing the top of the clough where a dramatic rock-shattered gulley is to the left.*
Below. *Blackden Barns and Clough from the start of the walk (Aug 27).*

Looking back into Blackden Clough from above the big waterfall (Aug 27)

Kinder Downfall via Crowden Clough and The Woolpacks

Entering the rock wonderland of the Woolpacks. Pym Chair is on the horizon, left.

This exhilarating, tough outing to the Peak District's most famous waterfall ascends wild Crowden Clough to the rocky viewpoint of Crowden Tower; meanders through the rock sculptures of the Woolpacks; visits the ever popular Downfall and returns across the barren Kinder Scout plateau, via Kinder Gates, to Grindslow Knoll and a scenic descent.

Length 16 kms / 10 miles **Map** O/S Explorer OL 1, *Dark Peak Area*, West Sheet
Start/Finish Lay-by car park just past the railway bridge on the minor road from Barber Booth to Upper Booth in the Vale of Edale (SK 107 847). The CP is marked on the map.
Refreshments Snacks and drinks at Upper Booth Farm, generally in summer.
Terrain There is rough, stony ground to the top of Crowden Clough and the brook has to be crossed a number of times before a short but steep ascent up a path or waterfall (see photo p.76) leads to the summit rocks of Crowden Tower. Map and compass skills required, especially for the crossing of Edale Moor to the head of Crowden Brook. There is an exceptionally steep, grassy descent (fine views) from Grindslow Knoll to the valley.
When To Go/What's There As with all routes on Kinder, it is best to go after a few dry days when the paths should be drier. However, The Downfall is at its best after a few days of heavy rain - so the choice is yours! After such rain and, in a strong westerly wind, The Downfall blows back high in the sky and is often observed 20 kms away in Oldham. Up close, this fountain is a magnificent sight, but a sudden change of wind direction may provide an instant drenching! In hard winters the waterfall freezes and is used by ice climbers as practise for more severe ascents (photo p.24). Many of the rock formations around the Woolpacks resemble Henry Moore sculptures and are well worth exploring. Small heath butterfly, emperor moth, mountain hare, kestrel, hen harrier, skylark, curlew, wheatear, snipe, heathers, "tundra" lichens, milkwort, cotton-grass and cloudberry may be spotted, and we once saw a grey squirrel eating lunch leftovers on Edale Rocks!
Nearby Edale Cross at SK 077 860 is there for strong walkers who want an extra 2 kms.

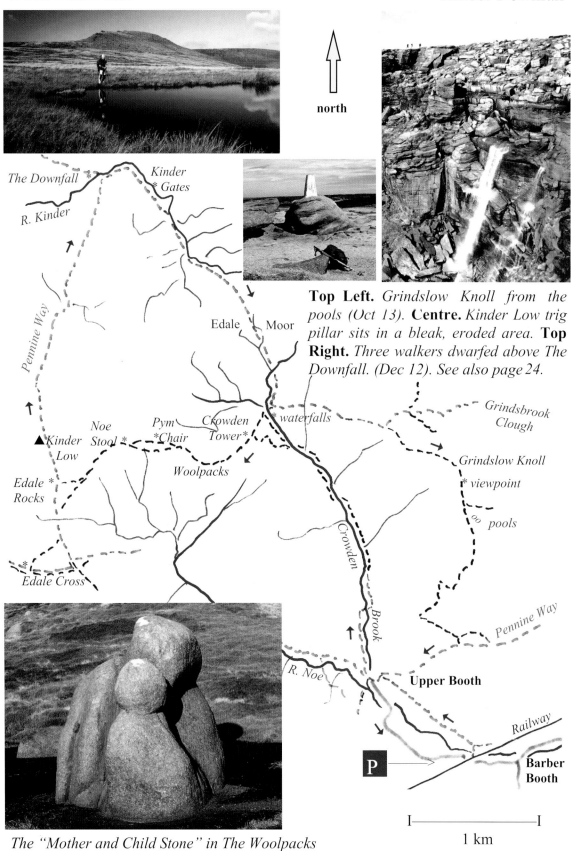

north

The Downfall ✳   *Kinder
* Gates

R. Kinder

Pennine Way

Edale   Moor

✳ *waterfalls*

*Grindsbrook
Clough*

*Noe
Stool* ✳   *Pym
Chair   *Crowden
Tower* ✳

▲ *Kinder
Low*

Grindslow Knoll

* *viewpoint*

Woolpacks

*Edale *
Rocks

oo *pools*

✳
Edale Cross

Crowden Brook

Pennine Way

R. Noe

Upper Booth

Railway

P ⟶

**Barber
Booth**

I————————I
1 km

Top Left. *Grindslow Knoll from the
pools (Oct 13).* **Centre.** *Kinder Low trig
pillar sits in a bleak, eroded area.* **Top
Right.** *Three walkers dwarfed above The
Downfall. (Dec 12). See also page 24.*

The "Mother and Child Stone" in The Woolpacks

74

Route Turn right out of the car park, walk down to the railway bridge and cross the river by the arched footbridge. Walk up to the track, go left and follow it as it becomes a path through fields and gates to **Upper Booth Farm**. Go left through the yard and right on the minor road for 50 metres. Turn right, through the stile and follow the left bank of **Crowden Brook** upstream until a second footbridge leads to the right bank (noting the water feature prior to the FB). Follow the path upstream, occasionally crossing the brook, to the summit waterfalls which provide scrambling. Once up, go left (west), pausing atop **Crowden Tower** for the view, before heading off to explore the weathered **Woolpacks** (with the winged **Pym Chair** above) and eventually the graffiti-adorned anvil-shaped **Noe Stool**. Onwards leads to the prominent blocks of **Edale Rocks**. Go right (north) for 300m to the trig pillar on **Kinder Low**. You are now on the **Pennine Way** and the way ahead leads to the busy **Downfall**. Turn right at the head of the fall and follow the shallow **River Kinder** upstream through **Kinder Gates**. Ahead, the main watercourse bears right at a cairn and later branches into a number of forks. Here, set compass to 160° and either thread your way through the drier groughs as they wriggle through the peat, or stagger up and down and over the tacky terrain in as straight a line as possible to emerge tired 1 km later near to the head of **Crowden Brook**. Cross the brook and follow the path nearest the edge as it runs east. Just after a short paved section and near a weathered split rock, keep ahead as the main path turns 90° left. You will see lines up to the prominent **Grindslow Knoll** (optional ascent) but our route follows the path that runs beneath the knoll. As it forks, keep right on the path that runs past two **pools** and up to a ruined wall. The path now plummets down to the right of a wall, crosses another path and falls to a stile. Another stile leads to the **Pennine Way** again, so go over it and follow the fields to **Upper Booth**. Go through the yard, and this time, turn left on the minor road leading back to the lay-by.

The shallow River Kinder passes through Kinder Gates, as you do, too (Dec 12).

Approaching the Noe Stool, with a couple enjoying an elevated lunch (June 29)

Scrambling up the top waterfalls of Crowden Clough (Aug 17). They can be avoided by using a steep path to the left. The path should be used when the waterfalls are in full spate or if the rocks are icy. Even the best walking footwear will have no grip on verglas.

11 Torrs Gorge Millennium Walkway and The Peak Forest Canal

The Millennium Walkway sweeps above the River Goyt in Torrs Gorge (June 12)

The award-winning Millennium Walkway in Torrs Gorge was created to link the Goyt Way with the Sett Valley Trail. We use it to link the Goyt Way with the Peak Forest Canal and to ramble through ancient industrial archaeology and enjoy some fine views as well.

Length 10 kms / 6.25 miles **Map** O/S Explorer OL 1, *Dark Peak Area*, West Sheet
Start/Finish Torr Top Street car park at SK 000 853, in New Mills. Follow brown signs off A6015 and B6101 to *Millennium Walkway*. Car park is Pay/Display (car reg.).
Terrain Well-defined paths and tracks all the way, together with a little roadwork.
Refreshments The welcoming *Fox Inn* is half way round. New Mills has the works.
When To Go/What's There A walk for all seasons. Torrs Gorge itself, hidden beneath New Mills, is a riot of viaducts, crags and weirs, where dipper and grey wagtail hunt. The majestic *Walkway* leads to the *Goyt Way* beside the river, and a wildlife pool with water-soldier (rare in The Peak), broad-leaved pondweed, frogs, newts and dragonflies - including common darter and brown hawker. Himalayan balsam is enveloping much of the river-bank. If you have kids, you pass through a playground at Hague Bar. From above, you can look over to *The Cage* folly in Lyme Park and to Sponds Hill (see below). Butterflies include speckled wood, comma, red admiral, gatekeeper, large skipper and painted lady. At Strines there is a fine hall and an ornate dovecote in the middle of a lake. You meet narrowboats, lift and swing bridges and New Mills Wharf on the Peak Forest Canal and, after the wharf, look out for the toxic giant hogweed plants, fortunately on the opposite bank. Canal-side plants include reed sweet-grass, yellow flag, meadowsweet, great willowherb and marsh woundwort. **Nearby** Lyme Park is worth a visit for its house, flowers, folly, deer and nearby *Bow Stones*. Follow the *Gritstone Trail* to the stones and on to views from Sponds Hill. Enter the park off the A6 near Disley, at SJ 965 843.

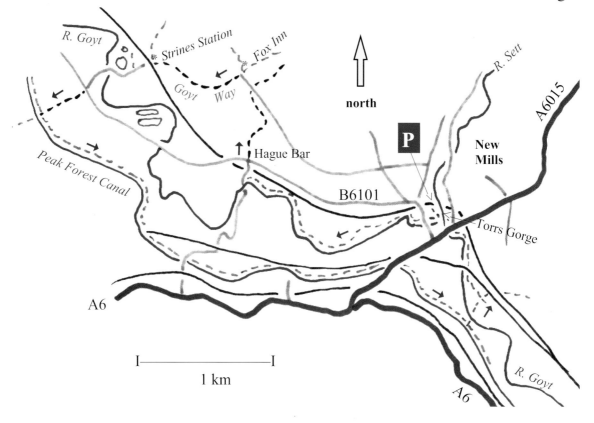

Watching a narrowboat chug by on the Peak Forest Canal (Sept 14)

Route Face the car park entrance then walk to and go through the opening in the top left corner of the CP. Turn left down the cobbles and then right at the former Chain Horse House (plaque) and down under a 4-arched viaduct to The **Torrs**. The R. Goyt is on your left and, ahead at a weir, is the river's confluence with the R. Sett. Follow the path right, go under another viaduct, ignoring steps right to the town centre, and cross the *Millennium Walkway*. Over, ignore FP on right and footbridge left and continue on the path through woodland beside the Goyt. The path joins a factory road which is crossed to enter the *Riverside Park*. Here, follow the left path and *Goyt Way* signs to a building and wall on the left. As the wall turns 90° left, you do, too. The path leads through scrub and woodland to a gate and stone step-stile. Go over and follow the path beside the river passing a *Midshires Way* sign (only 210 miles to *The Ridgeway*!) to a kissing-gate. The riverside path leads to another gate and an entrance gate to the wildlife pond on the right. There is another gate after the pond and in another 50m turn right up wooden steps to the playground at **Hague Bar**. Turn right, cross the railway bridge to the **B6101**, cross and go up Hague Fold Road, with Toll Bar Cottage (1840) on your left. The road soon becomes a pleasant, metalled lane and, after dwellings, a sandy track leads up to another metalled lane. Turn left to the **Fox Inn**. Just before it, the *Goyt Way* leads left down a shady track and under a bridge at **Strines Station**. Soon the Goyt Way turns right, but we continue on past Strines Hall on the left and the dovecote lake on the right and over the R. Goyt to the B6101 again at Strines Road. Cross and go up the track ahead to just before a bridge with a curved facade where wooden steps on the right lead up to the **Peak Forest Canal**. Turn left and follow the towpath for about 5 kms, at the end of which an aromatic sweet factory precedes New Mills Wharf. Leave the towpath just before Bridge No 29 (plate), ignore the riverside park gate and walk ahead on the path which leaves the canal on the right and runs downhill to a footbridge over the **R. Goyt**. Turn left to a farm and left again at a junction. Walk the farm track to the **R. Sett** and go under a viaduct. Leave the track at a path on the left to follow the river under a two-tiered viaduct and over a footbridge to the Torrs.

On the Millennium Walkway (Sept 14)

Through a viaduct in Torrs Gorge (Sept 14)

The dovecote in the lake at Strines (June 12)
Inset. *Beside the River Goyt (July 21)*

12 Roych Clough, Brown Knoll, South Head and Mount Famine

South Head from the path to Breckhead (Feb 15)

Viewed from The Knott (Walk 8) or William Clough, South Head and Mount Famine are shapely, enticing hills. As well as ascending these fine viewpoints, this rugged hike also ascends scenic Roych Clough to Brown Knoll, where aircraft remains have a story to tell.

Length 14 kms / 8.75 miles **Map** O/S Explorer OL1, *Dark Peak Area*, West Sheet
Start/Finish A lay-by on the north side of the B6062, about 100 metres north of where the A624 turns right under a railway bridge, 1 km east of Chinley at SK 051 824.
Terrain A fairly tough walk on a mixture of stony tracks, paths over the moors and an uphill ascent of Roych Clough, off-path and on rough pasture. A little roadwork, too.
Refreshments The *Crown and Mitre* at the start and end of the walk.
When To Go/What's There A walk for all seasons, but not after heavy snowfall. A small courtyard at the start of the walk unusually has a number of gravestones embedded in it. The remains of an Oxford HN594 that came down in the winter of 1945 lies near to the trig pillar on Brown Knoll (GPS 08183 85201). The three air crew survived the crash and, after wrapping his more injured colleagues in parachutes, Ted Croker crawled, with sprained ankles, 2 kms down to the valley for help. He later became Secretary of The Football Association! A memorial plate on the summit rocks of Mount Famine bears a warning; "*Never Walk Alone*" and two window lintels in the barn of Beet Farm also bear inscriptions, one of which poses an even starker warning: "*He that walketh with wisemen shall be wise : but a companion of fools shall be destroyed*"! And, if you've skeletons in the cupboard, don't read the other! Brown hare, partridge, curlew and skylark inhabit the lower pastures; golden plover, mountain hare and peregrine falcon the upper heights. Beet Lane supports foxgloves, lichen walls and a view to a gorse-clad valley. The *Shake Holes* on the map are overgrown *Sphagna* pools. **Nearby** *The Chestnut Centre* has otters.

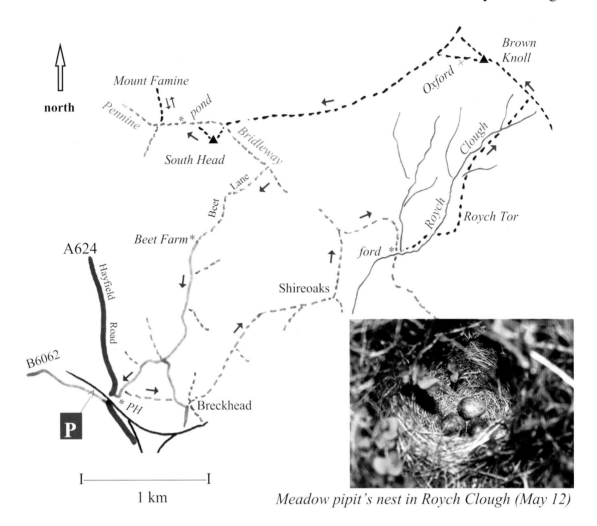

Meadow pipit's nest in Roych Clough (May 12)

Wreckage of the Oxford on Brown Knoll (May 12)

Route Walk back to the **A624**, follow it under the railway bridge and cross the road to the *Crown and Mitre* **PH**. Take the lane immediately left of the pub; follow it as it bends 90° left, then turn first right soon after. A few metres up the lane on the right is the small courtyard of gravestones. About 20 metres on, turn up the steps to the narrow, walled path leading to a stile. Over, walk ahead through fields, keeping close to the wall on the left, to wall steps. Although it may look intrusive, this is the right of way, so go over the steps and take the left path to the drive and on to a minor road at **Breckhead**. Turn right then soon left up a farm entrance. Walk ahead to meet a track signed *Shireoaks*. About 1 km up the track a small building dated 1930 appears on the left (*Resr* on O/S map) and ahead the hamlet of **Shireoaks**. Walk through the hamlet and then go through the gate to the left of the last building. The path ahead leads to a track which is the **Pennine Bridleway**. Turn right, signed *Perryfoot*, and follow the track down to the **ford** in the valley bottom. Ford the first stream (seat, poem?), then turn left at the gate and go up through the gap in the walls (access sign) into **Roych Clough**. Cross to the right bank of the stream at your convenience and slant up to the right, to arrive below the foot of the crags of **Roych Tor**, where easier going leads on to the top of the clough. Here, angle slightly to the left and walk ahead to meet a conspicuous, peaty path which, by turning left on it, leads to the trig pillar on **Brown Knoll**. From here, walk for about a minute on a bearing of 296° to the remains of the **Oxford**, which lie in a shallow, peaty depression. Now angle slightly left and head down the moor to a fence, which has access stiles identified by taller posts. Cross the fence and turn left down the path to reach the Pennine Bridleway again. Ahead, a path rises to the summit cairn on **South Head**. From

the summit a path leads NW down to the bridleway. Here, turn left and, just after stone gateposts, turn right up the path to the summit rocks of **Mount Famine**. Return to the bridleway, turn left, pass the **pond** on the left and keep on the bridleway, through a gate to reach a track junction on the right. This is **Beet Lane** (currently signposted). Turn right, down the track to reach the inscriptions on the barn lintels at **Beet Farm**, after about one km. The track now becomes a metalled lane, which is followed all the way down to the start of the walk, and the welcoming sight of the *Crown and Mitre*.

On the summit rocks of Mount Famine (Feb 17)

Mount Famine from the summit cairn on South Head (Oct 3)

Roych Clough from Shireoaks (Feb 17)

Walks On Dark Peak Map —————— East Sheet

(Explorer Outdoor Leisure Series No 01)

There are many attractive hummocks in the Woodlands Valley formed by landslips long ago - similar to those which created Alport Castles (Walk 17) and swept away the road beneath Mam Tor (Walk 21). These areas are composed of unstable strata of shale, grit and sandstone. The hummocks can be seen on the left as you drive north-west up the valley or from Walk 17 (Oct 27). Abbey Clough (Walk 16) reveals another huge landslip.

Upper Derwent via Linch Clough, Barrow Stones and Crow Stones

Descending to the valley from the top of Broadhead Clough (Nov 9)

This long hill-walk is a classic of the Dark Peak, being a circuit of the best scenery and rock formations of The Derwent watershed. The path in the valley which follows the river can be used as an escape route or as an easier walk. Stock the rucksacks and start early.

Length 16 kms / 10 miles **Map** O/S Explorer OL1, *Dark Peak Area*, East Sheet **Start/Finish** The King's Tree (SK 167 938). This parking area (not on the map) is at the end of the minor road that leaves the A57 at Ashopton Viaduct (SK 191 864) and meanders for 12 kms (7.5 miles) beside Ladybower, Derwent and Howden reservoirs. **Terrain** A tough walk, mostly on high, faint moorland paths together with some pathless moor. A few bogs. Map/compass skills essential in mist. **Refreshments** None on route. **When To Go/What's There** Best when the heather is out, but dramatic all year. Near the fabulous rock sculptures at the Barrow Stones a Labrador-tea shrub flourishes amidst stands of bilberry. The white flowers appear in June/July. Here, we also found a dead mole! Another unusual sight was a mountain hare being chased by a stoat. Birds include goshawk, kestrel, peregrine falcon, golden plover, curlew, grey wagtail and, in winter, crossbills and goldcrests may be observed in the treetops. Tiger beetles and lizards can be seen on the lower paths but red squirrels are now a very rare sight among the larches and pines. Wreckage of the Consul TF-RPM en route to Iceland which came down in April 1951 killing all 3 on board, is met on Crow Stones Edge. **Nearby** The war memorial relocated to SK 182 883 is a remnant of the village of Derwent which, like Ashopton, was drowned to create Ladybower Reservoir. The dams are immortalised by real and celluloid exploits. **Note.** The road from Fairholmes CP (SK172 893) to The King's Tree is closed Sundays and Bank Holidays, when a bus operates. First buses about 09.30 but call the Information Centre on 01433 650953. If you miss the last bus back it is an additional 5 mile walk to Fairholmes! So best go by car for a first visit. There is talk of a road toll...

Mountain hare tracks on Round Hill (Jan 11). Horse Stone Naze is above the walker and Shepherds Meeting Stones upper left of picture. A desolate place in winter. **Inset.** *Larval skin of common hawker dragonfly found at the pond below Round Hill.*

Looking back at the wonderful Crow Stones (Aug 16)

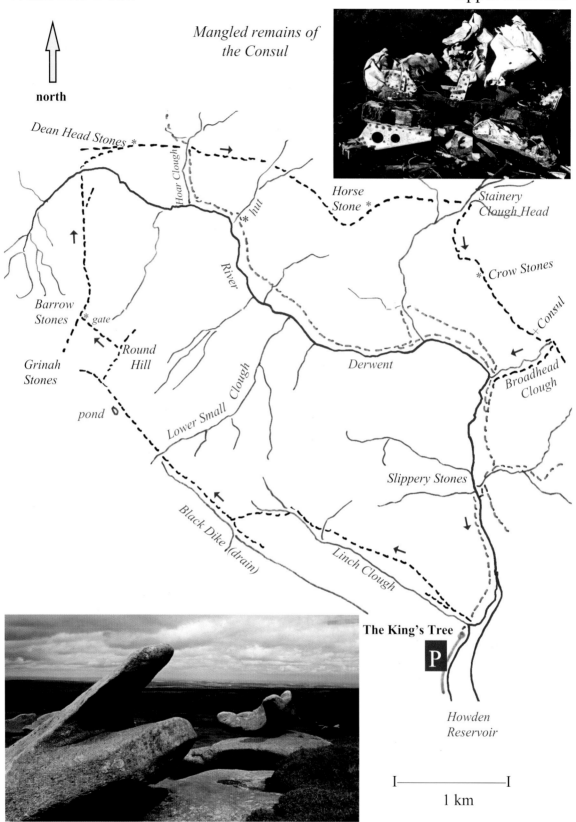

north

Mangled remains of the Consul

Dean Head Stones *

Hoar Clough

Horse Stone

Stainery Clough Head

* hut

River

* Crow Stones

Barrow Stones

* gate

Round Hill

+ Consul

Derwent

Grinah Stones

Broadhead Clough

pond

Lower Small Clough

Slippery Stones

Black Dike (drain)

Linch Clough

The King's Tree

P

Howden Reservoir

I————————I
1 km

Rock sculptures at the Barrow Stones (Aug 16). It is a fine place for a walkabout.

Route After a peek at the commemorative stone beneath **The King's Tree** itself, go through the gate, cross the stream and immediately turn left on a faint path up the wood to reach a gate and NT sign for **Linch Clough**. Once over, don't walk the path ahead but take the narrow path just right which rises up the right hand spine of the clough. The gradient eventually eases and the way leads on just below the heather/bilberry bank for about a km to the head of the clough. Here, is a shallow, inviting watercourse to the right but the main path keeps left, and is followed until it joins another path at a boggy area. Turn right and follow this path on the right bank of a choked drain (**Black Dike**), with the **Grinah Stones** now ahead, across a grough and past a **pond**, after which our path swings right to ascend **Round Hill**. Turn left at the cairn on the top and walk uphill to a **gate** beneath the **Barrow Stones**. After exploring, follow the edge path down to a "stile" at the conservation fence. Cross and walk north down the moor to the fledgling **River Derwent**. Step across and slant right (no path) uphill to meet a path leading rightwards to the scattered **Dean Head Stones**. A way leads on from beneath the last outcrop to the Shepherds Meeting Stones at the head of **Hoar Clough**. (Here, a path leads down just left of the clough to the valley path and a tin **hut**). The high path leads 2 kms over the moor to reach the **Horse Stone**, which looks more like horse droppings than the animal itself. From here the path loops around **Stainery Clough Head** to reach the distinctive **Crow Stones** (beneath are the *Rocking Stones*, but few do). About 200 m after the Crow Stones the path forks at more rocks. Take the right fork along the edge and the path leads straight to remains of the **Consul**, where there is also a line of grouse butts at 90° to the path. Another 200 m or so on, another line of grouse butts are met. Now turn right and soon a path leads downhill, just to the left of the butts and watercourse (which leads to **Broadhead Clough**). Further down the path widens and runs pleasantly down to the path in the valley. Turn left, cross the footbridge dedicated to Fred Heardman, visionary of the Edale Mountain Rescue Team, and cross the packhorse bridge at **Slippery Stones** over the R. Derwent. The bridge was relocated here from the village of Derwent and there is a commemoration stone to John Derry in the bridge wall. From here, a track leads south back to the parking area.

Looking out from Dean Head Stones (Sept 21)

14 Howden Edge, Margery Hill and Howden Reservoir

On Howden Edge (Aug 27). **Inset.** *A rock at Margery Stones resembles a turtles head.*

A waterside stroll beside the length of Howden Reservoir is followed by an ascent of Row Top to Howden Edge. The edge path leads to the trig pillar on Margery Hill and an optional detour to a major WWII aircraft crash. We descend by the old path of Cut Gate.

Length 15 kms / 9.4 miles **Map** O/S Explorer OL1, *Dark Peak Area*, East Sheet
Note. If you visit the *Stirling* wreck, you will extend the route by a further 2.5 kms
Start/Finish The King's Tree (SK 167 938). Information as per Walk 13.
Terrain Low level tracks followed by paths up and over rough terrain and a stony path for the descent to Slippery Stones. The optional detour threads through mature heather.
Refreshments None on route, so stock the rucksack for this quite tough venture.
When To Go/What's There Wreckage of the Stirling LJ628 which crashed on 21 July 1944 lies above Stainery Clough. The crew of ten were lucky to survive and, if you visit the site, it makes you realise what tough terrain the uninjured had to wade through to get help. Birds include cormorant and common sandpiper at the reservoir; lapwing, wheatear, skylark and curlew on the rough pastures and buzzard and kestrel in the air. In summer, common hawker dragonflies breed in the boggy flushes and mate in the heather; through which mountain hares prance and emperor moths jiggle. Flushes beneath the edge raise bog pondweed, water-crowfoot, cotton-grass and the scarce creeping spearwort. Lizards, mining bees, tiger and rove beetles may be seen on the sandy paths. Hen harriers have successfully bred locally and attempts are being made to reintroduce black grouse. Small heath is the most profuse butterfly and Margery Hill raises stands of cross-leaved heath. Late summer is a good time to spot the bee-mimicking large, black bee-fly. Minninglow Hill can be seen due south from High Stones. **Nearby** Pike Lowe is now on access land so park at Langsett (SE 201 011); follow Mickleden Edge; cut across Lost Lad (another!) to Pike Lowe. Descend via Round Hole and Thickwoods Brook to North America!

Above. *Taking a bearing at the trig pillar on Margery Hill to the Stirling remains above Stainery Clough (Aug 27). The two sites are situated at 20230 /95606 and 20144/95525 (GPS references).*

Middle. *Mountain hare tracks in the snow above Howden Edge crossed by those of (possibly) a field mouse (March 8). Quite a size differential!*

Below. *Undercarriage and other remains of the Stirling lie in the heather (Aug 27). See also p.32.*

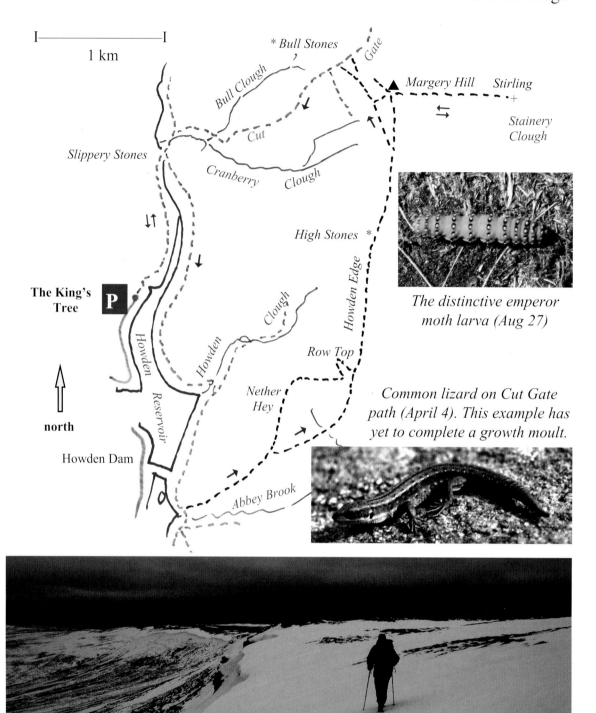

1 km

* Bull Stones

Gate

▲ Margery Hill   Stirling

Bull Clough

Cut

Cranberry   Clough

Slippery Stones

High Stones *

Stainery
Clough

The King's
Tree

P

Howden Edge

Clough

Row Top

Howden

Howden

Reservoir

Nether
Hey

north

Howden Dam

Abbey Brook

*The distinctive emperor
moth larva (Aug 27)*

*Common lizard on Cut Gate
path (April 4). This example has
yet to complete a growth moult.*

Heading into an early spring storm above the cornices on Howden Edge (March 8)

Route Walk past the oak **King's Tree** (planted 25/09/45, plaque), go through the gate ahead and follow the track for about 1½ kms to **Slippery Stones**. Go over the bridge, bear left and soon sharp right on the cycle track and footpath signed to the *Derwent Valley*. Follow the track through a few gates for about 3½ kms beside the east bank of **Howden Reservoir** to the towers and headwall of **Howden Dam**. About 200m on, turn left up the concession track to a gate and a NT sign to **Nether Hey**, together with *Access Land* sign. Walk up and through a second gate (*CPRE Merit Award* stone) and then through a third gate. The track ahead is now across rough pasture. About 100m past the third gate the track forks, and you have a choice of ways to and up **Row Top**. The left and more worn track follows the O/S map route which meanders to Row Top, but the right fork leads to a more direct route and narrow path up the shoulder of Row Top, which has a "false summit" before the paths join. The incline now relents and the path soon leads on to the highest point on the route, **High Stones**. The level path ahead follows the crags along **Howden Edge**. As the crags diminish you will see rocks to the right of the edge. These are the Margery Stones. Although paths soon lead off to them, it is best to stay on the path along the edge until you are just past the boulders, then turn right up a narrow path to the trig pillar on **Margery Hill**. To visit the **Stirling** crash site, set compass to 96° east and about 20-30 minutes graft should see you there. Return to the trig pillar and also return the same way to the edge path. This will avoid the fenced-off Margery Hill Cairn, which archaeologists think may be a 3,500 year-old Bronze Age site. Not too much visible evidence, though. The path ahead rounds the fencing and leads on to a fork, where the left path is the shorter route to the ancient pathway of **Cut Gate**. Turn left, and follow this path all the way down as it first leads over paving then spirals down to the valley. Here, ford the stream emanating from **Bull Clough** and cross the brook from **Cranberry Clough** by the footbridge to reach Slippery Stones, and the track back to the King's Tree parking area.

Slippery Stones and The Upper Derwent from the relocated packhorse bridge (Aug 27)

15 Rocher Wood, Agden Side and Dale Dike Reservoir

The route passes High Bradfield church of St Nicholas (Sept 3)

A quite complex but very rewarding outing to the reservoirs and scenery of the Bradfield and Agden regions in the north-east of the National Park. It also visits Low and High Bradfield, Rocher Wood Crags for an outstanding view and the site of a national tragedy.

Length 12 kms / 7.5 miles **Map** O/S Explorer OL1, *Dark Peak Area*, East Sheet
Start/Finish The Sands car park off Fair House Lane, Low Bradfield at SK 262 920
Follow the "Recycling" logo signs. A playground is attached to the CP with PCs nearby.
Terrain Quite a tough walk on paths, tracks and open pastures. Falls from the top of Rocher Wood Crags would be fatal and care has to be taken on some steep, downhill paths. Minor roads are crossed and there is 1km of walking on pathless Blindside Lane.
Refreshments *Old Horns Inn* High Bradfield; *The Plough* or tea rooms Low Bradfield.
When To Go/What's There A walk for all seasons. Ancient stone gateposts abound. Upper Bradfield has stocks, *VR* letterbox, topiary plus gargoyles on the church. Britain's worst ever reservoir disaster happened in 1864 when the earthen headwall of Dale Dike collapsed, drowning 244 people in the Loxley and Don Valleys. Plants include cowwheat beside the path at Bailey Hill, bell and ling heather, harebell, hawkweeds, tansy, wood sorrel, creeping cinquefoil, foxglove, and knapweed, plus nut-bearing hazels. A bog pond raises cotton-grass, *Sphagnum* moss, black darter dragonfly and large red damselfly. There are meadow grasshoppers and wall, gatekeeper, small heath and small copper butterflies, and the odd emperor moth in the heather. Goldcrests inhabit the pines and pink-foot geese are frequently seen on Agden Res. In summer, you can watch bowls and cricket, too. **Nearby** is a footpath to Boots Folly (p.24) and its commanding view over Strines Reservoir. A little further north, you could devise a walk to include Hurkling Edge, Flint Hill, Ewden Beck Stone Circle (SK 238 966) and Canyards Hills, all of which are now on access land. The circle is signed from the path opposite Broomhead Hall.

Kitting-up before a storm hits Dale Dike Reservoir (June 22)

Looking down on Agden Reservoir from Rocher Wood Crags (Nov 26)

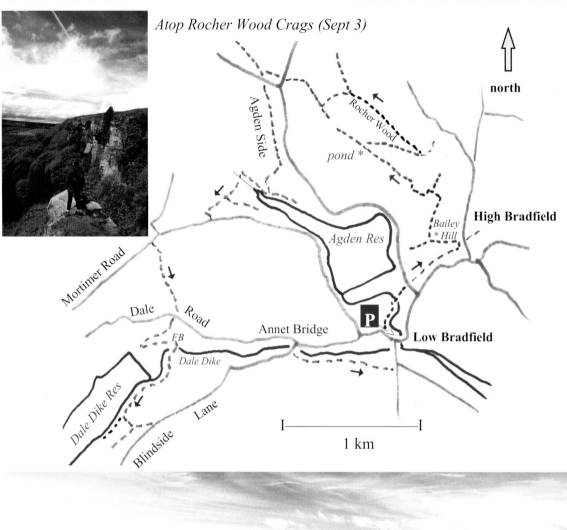

Atop Rocher Wood Crags (Sept 3)

Looking towards Strines Reservoir from above Rocher Wood Crags (Aug7)

Route Take the path left of the car park entrance, ignore a footbridge on the right but walk ahead on ancient slabs and cross the stream by a second footbridge. A flight of stone steps leads uphill to a path that runs to a road. Cross and go up to a wooden stile. Over, keep straight ahead and then angle up left to a gate, with **High Bradfield** church now in view. Head to the start of the castellated wall beneath the church and walk (with the *Old Horns Inn* ahead, right) to the church gates at Towngate. Turn left on the path to ***Bailey Hill***. Walk through the graveyards to a stone opening. A path right leads up to the bailey if you're interested, but the route keeps ahead down the wood, turns 90° left to reach a gate, crosses Rocher End Brook to reach another gate. Here, turn right and go through the right set of gateposts (waymarks) and up to a pylon. Turn left through the opening in the wall and head across the meadow to reach stone step stile on left. Don't go over but go through the opening to the right in the direction of the crags ahead and pass the bog **pond** on the left. About 100m after, turn sharp right at a waymark post (a ladder stile reached means you've gone too far). The path is indistinct through the bracken but soon opens out and leads up a flight of steps and joins a farm track. About 70m on, turn sharp left up to a faint path to a fence and follow the path as it now runs above **Rocher Wood** Crags, being careful not to trip over the climbers belay posts! There's a gate halfway along and at the end of the edge the path bends to the left and then runs steeply down through rough pasture to a stile in the bottom left corner of the field. Turn right on the track and walk to a road. Cross, enter field and go to ladder stile on left and another road. Cross and take the FP (No 140) which runs across **Agden Side** (seat) before turning right to run steeply downhill (care here) to a stile and better path to **Agden Reservoir**. Turn right (seat), ignore footbridge left, pass Agden Bog NR on right and follow path left across Agden Dike via bridge and uphill to a seat and stone gateposts. Keep ahead at this path junction and walk through the wood on the path that swings left, crosses a stream and reaches a minor road. Turn right and go up to a road junction. Turn left and soon left down the bridleway (No 40) to stile/gate. Keep ahead down the farmland track and then path (views to Boots Folly) as it runs down to a gate and track to a road. Turn right and soon left over a stile. Past the information board take the left fork and the path crosses **Dale Dike** by a **FB** to steps left of pipe outlets. More steps lead to a

path through the pines and the beginning of **Dale Dike Reservoir**. After about 300m, turn left up the path through the wood, keeping left at a junction to reach a road, which is **Blindside Lane**. Turn left and follow it for about one kilometre to just before **Annet Bridge**, where a stone step stile on the right leads to a path that runs over fields and a wall stile to become a track to a road. Here there are views up to unusual Ughill Hall. Turn left to **Low Bradfield**, passing (or entering) *The Plough* on the right on route back to the car park.

The bog pool beneath Rocher Wood (Aug 7)

16 Derwent Edge, Back Tor and Abbey Clough

On the path to Back Tor. **Inset.** *Peregrine falcon kill above Abbey Clough (both Nov 20)*

The longest walk in the book - but what an outing! A stroll beside Ladybower Reservoir is followed by a rise to Derwent Edge with its commanding views and quirky rock formations of the Wheel Stones, Salt Cellar and Cakes of Bread. Back Tor summit leads to the path high above Abbey Brook and arguably the wildest scenery in the Dark Peak.

Length 17 kms / 10.63 miles **Map** O/S Explorer OL1, *Dark Peak Area*, East Sheet
Start/Finish Fairholmes car park (fee), visitor centre and cycle hire, SK 173 893
Terrain All the paths are easy to follow but stretches of the path along Derwent Edge and beyond become boggy after heavy rain. There is a steady climb up to Derwent Edge.
Refreshments Occasional (mainly weekend) take away café at the visitor centre.
When To Go/What's There A walk for all seasons, but Derwent Edge can be a ferocious place in winter. The interest starts in the car park, where a totem pole of local wildlife and similarly carved picnic tables await. The majestic stonework of Derwent Dam is a testament to lost skills, and the headwall becomes an awesome waterfall when the dam overflows. Information boards recount its construction. Towards the edge is a shelter and seat with carved curlew heads. There is a natural cave bivouac (and winter lunch haven) down a short gully at the end of Dovestone Tor - it holds four comfortably. Mountain hare, goshawk, peregrine falcon, golden plover, curlew and skylark are on high ground; treecreeper, woodpecker, nuthatch and squirrel the woods. Reservoir verges support milkwort, trefoils, figwort and lady's-mantle. The moors are breathtaking when the heather flowers. Emperor moths can be seen flitting erratically over the purple heath and black darter dragonflies breed in boggy pools. There are some ancient, carved boulders beside the upper reaches of Abbey Brook. On the descent of Abbey Clough you look down on waterfalls far below and pass a major landslip hillock. **Nearby** *The Seven Stones of Hordron* (p.19) and the pinnacle *Head Stone* (SK 256 873) are on access land.

Below Right. *The ancient carvings on some boulders at the head of Abbey Brook were recorded on 15/09/06. The unusual symbols are currently being evaluated by local archaeologists.*

Above. *The Salt Cellar (Aug 12). Not too many walkers attempt the overhang to stand on top!* **Above Right.** *Entering the dry cave bivouac at Dovestone Tor in torrential rain.*

On the path above dramatic Abbey Clough (Sept 8)

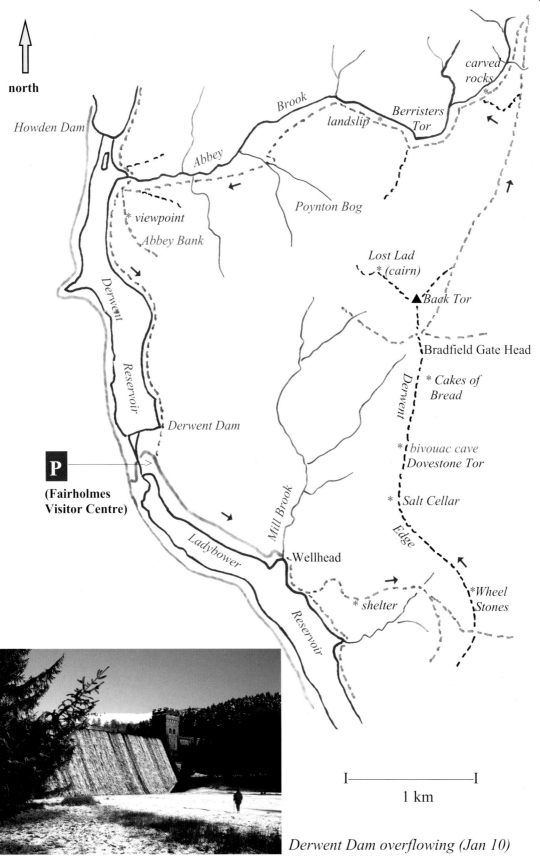

north

Howden Dam

Brook

Abbey

viewpoint

Abbey Bank

Derwent

Reservoir

Derwent Dam

P

**(Fairholmes
Visitor Centre)**

Ladybower

Mill Brook

Reservoir

Poynton Bog

landslip *

*carved
rocks*

*

Berristers
Tor

Lost Lad
* (cairn)

▲Back Tor

Bradfield Gate Head

* Cakes of
Bread

Derwent

* bivouac cave
Dovestone Tor

* Salt Cellar

Edge

Wellhead

* shelter

*Wheel
Stones

I———————————I

1 km

Derwent Dam overflowing (Jan 10)

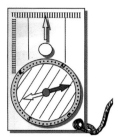

Route Turn right out of the car park and take the road which initially runs parallel to the headwall of **Derwent Dam** before swinging right to follow the eastern shore of **Ladybower Reservoir**. About 300 metres after the conspicuous inlet at **Wellhead**, leave the road on the left at the footpath sign to *Moscar*. The rising path runs between buildings and beyond up to a path junction at a gate. Walk ahead here on the path which leads up to the main path along **Derwent Edge**. Turn left and soon the **Wheel Stone**s are reached. Onwards leads to the Salt Cellar and later Dovestone Tor. The **Salt Cellar** is a little below the path and partially obscured from view - so if you reach the steps to **Dovestone Tor** and the NT sign, you've missed it! At the end of Dovestone Tor, the weathered crags of which lie below the path over Derwent Edge, is a **bivouac cave** down a short gully on the left. Also worth a look is Dovestone Tor Crag for the effects of erosion on rock. Onwards, the **Cakes of Bread** are on the right and, soon after, a path crosses at right angles at a signpost. From here, our way ahead leads to the trig pillar at **Back Tor** where the rocks are generously carved with graffiti, including the almost weathered-away engagement of Jack and Mary. If you're tired, you could descend to the valley from here via **Lost Lad** (a cairn on a hillock). But, as the best is yet to come, follow the path which runs in a northerly direction from Back Tor for about 2 kms, until a conspicuous scattering of boulders is reached. Here, a distinct path leads sharp left downhill off the main path to a small rocky outcrop and on down to meet another path running high above **Abbey Brook**. If you want to see the **carved rocks**, turn right for about 50 m, otherwise turn left and follow the path all the way down past fabulous scenery to within 40 metres of **Derwent Reservoir**. If you're not spent, you could ascend 200 m up the path on the left to the viewpoint on **Abbey Bank**. Whatever, turn left on the waterside track back to Fairholmes.

The Wheel Stones with male red grouse in the foreground (Aug 12)

17   Bellhag Tor, Alport Castles and Blackley Hey Wood

Looking to the crumbling rocks of The Tower at Alport Castles (Feb 12)

This trip to the great landslip of the Peak District takes the easiest ascent to Bellhag Tor, from where easy walking leads to Alport Castles and the views. Optional closer looks at The Tower or the wildlife pool beneath The Tower are possible from the descent path, which leads to The Woodlands Valley, the River Ashop and through Blackley Hey Wood.

Length 11 kms / 6.9 miles **Map** O/S Explorer OL1, *Dark Peak Area*, East Sheet
Start/Finish Off-road parking area 50 metres south and on the opposite side of the road to the signed entrance to Hagg Farm Centre, off the A57 at SK 162 885
Terrain Well-defined paths and tracks, a few of which are stony and slippery when wet. Detours for a closer look at The Tower or the pond are off-path and over rough land.
Refreshments None on route. *Ladybower Inn* and *Yorkshire Bridge Inn* not far away.
When To Go/What's There The landslip is a wonderful piece of nature whatever the season, and along the way there are extensive views to The Great Ridge, Kinder Scout, Bleaklow, Winhill Pike, Derwent Edge and Ladybower. After nearly being persecuted to extinction in The Peak, the peregrine falcon regained a foothold by breeding at The Castles. Ravens breed here, too and kestrels float motionless on the up-currents from the Woodlands Valley. Oak and hard fern, together with broom, cross-leaved heath and a rare hawkweed are found at The Castles. The woods have liverworts, wood sorrel, wood basil, bluebell, foxglove and numerous fungi. In summer, lizards, rove and tiger beetles, and emperor moth larvae may cross your path, and on the way down from The Castles, meadow grasshoppers abound. Small heath butterflies are abundant and, if you visit the pond on a sunny day in August, dragonflies should include black darter, common hawker and emerald damselfly. Stonechat, common sandpiper, and heron visit the River Ashop.
Nearby on Rowlee Pasture lie a few remains of the Defiant which crashed in April 1941 (GPS SK 155 905). The crew parachuted to safety. There's the odd mountain hare, too.

Rowlee Bridge and the River Ashop from the path to Blackley Hey Wood (Sept 4)

Determining a GPS reference at the Defiant remains on Rowlee Pasture (Nov 1).
To find these scant remains, walk on a bearing of 80° from the highest point on the paved
path (point 483m on O/S map) for about 400m down unfriendly tussocks. Then return...

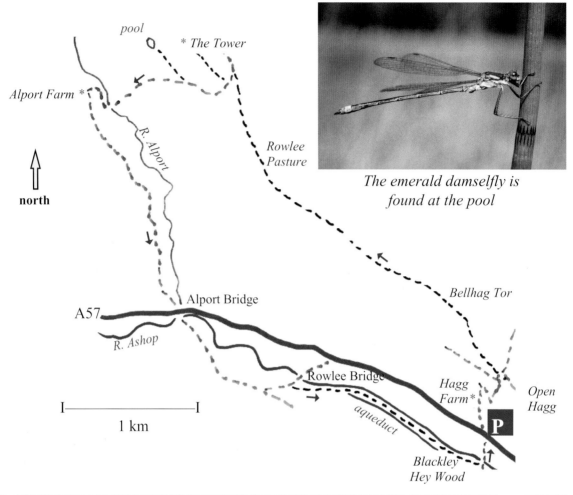

The emerald damselfly is
found at the pool

Approaching the pool in the landslips beneath The Tower (Aug 7)
Inset. *Fly Agaric beside the path to Blackley Hey Wood (Oct 15)*

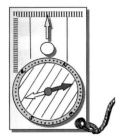

Route Turn left out of the parking area and walk up the road for about 30 metres. Cross the **A57** and walk up the bridleway that leads to the **Hagg Farm** Environmental Education Centre. As the track swings left to the centre, keep ahead through a gate. The track becomes stony, and spirals uphill, through another gate to a gate with stile near the top. About 20m beyond, turn left off the track up some wooden steps. Cross another track, and go to a ladder stile and gate at a wall. Follow the grassy path ahead to another stile. You are now above **Bellhag Tor** and the views are expansive. From here, the path follows rough ground across **Rowlee Pasture**, and eventually a paved section rises sedately through the moor grass. This stretch is your best chance of spotting a short-eared owl. A wet plod leads to drier terrain and Alport Castles. Walk on until you are level with **The Tower** below. Here are natural seats and views. Retrace your steps for about 100m and turn right down the narrow path that leads to the left of landslips. (To view The Tower closer, go through the gap on the right, a few metres down the path). Further down, after two stiles, the wall on the right turns 90° right. The way is now clear for a visit to the **pool**. Return, follow the path down to the **River Alport**. Cross the footbridge and turn right, through stiles, to **Alport Farm**. Turn left down the drive. After about 1½ kms, turn left off the track at a right bend, and a stile leads to the A57 at **Alport Bridge**. Cross the road and the **River Ashop** via the ford or footbridge and turn left on a track. This rises to Blackley Hey and eventually joins a metalled track. Onwards; at a fork, keep left downhill (signposted *Upper Derwent*). Before the track descends to **Rowlee Bridge**, turn right off the track and on to a path (signposted *Ladybower and Bamford*) which soon runs left of an aqueduct and through **Blackley Hey Wood**. Here, the path passes a circular inspection shaft, joins another path and runs down to Haggwater Bridge. Cross the bridge over the River Ashop; walk up the stony track to the A57 and turn right for the parking area.

Across Rowlee Pasture with Derwent Edge, (Walk 16), on the skyline (Feb 12).

18 Lockerbrook , Crook Hill and Ladybower Reservoir

The rocky summit of Crook Hill (July 20)

Like Oker Hill (Walk 48), Crook Hill is lower than the surrounding terrain, but the reward is a fine 360° view. The walk rises to Lockerbrook for views of the Woodlands Valley and The Great Ridge; crosses airy Bridge-end Pasture to Crook Hill for views of Kinder, Derwent Edge and Bamford Edge, before descending for an easy waterside stroll.

Length 10 kms / 6.25 miles **Map** O/S Explorer OL1, *Dark Peak Area*, East Sheet
Start/Finish Lay-by about 300 metres south of Fairholmes Visitor Centre (and cycle hire) at SK 173 889. This lay-by soon fills up as it's free. If full, park at Fairholmes (fee)
Terrain Straightforward walking on well-defined paths and tracks, but the ascent of Crook Hill is off-path over uneven ground, and care has to be taken at the rocky summits.
Refreshments Weekend take-away snack-bar at Fairholmes Visitor Centre.
When To Go/What's There A walk for all seasons. The woods up to Lockerbrook are home to goldcrest, crossbill and, in autumn, many species of fungi. Hare, curlew and skylark frequent Bridge-end Pasture, and buzzard and peregrine falcon are often observed on high. Goshawks perform seasonal courtship over Ladybower, whose waters support cormorants and goosanders as well as the ubiquitous mallards, tufted duck and Canada geese. When the water level is very low, some ruins of the village of Derwent may become exposed, but the church steeple was sadly demolished. The War Memorial saved from drowning Derwent, stands beside the road to the lay-by. Stoats flit in and out of gritstone walls near Open Hagg. The roadside banks approaching Fairholmes support bluebells in spring and the waterside verges support heath bedstraw, common and heath milkwort and foxgloves. The *Salt Cellar* and *Wheel Stones* (Walk 16) are visible above.
Nearby Don't miss the wonderful viewpoint from Whinstone Lee Tor (SK 197 874) and there is currently a "Dambusters" Exhibition in the west tower of Derwent Dam.

On the descent from Crook Hill to Ladybower, with Derwent Edge above (Feb 8)

Approaching the twin peaks of Crook Hill (Aug 22)

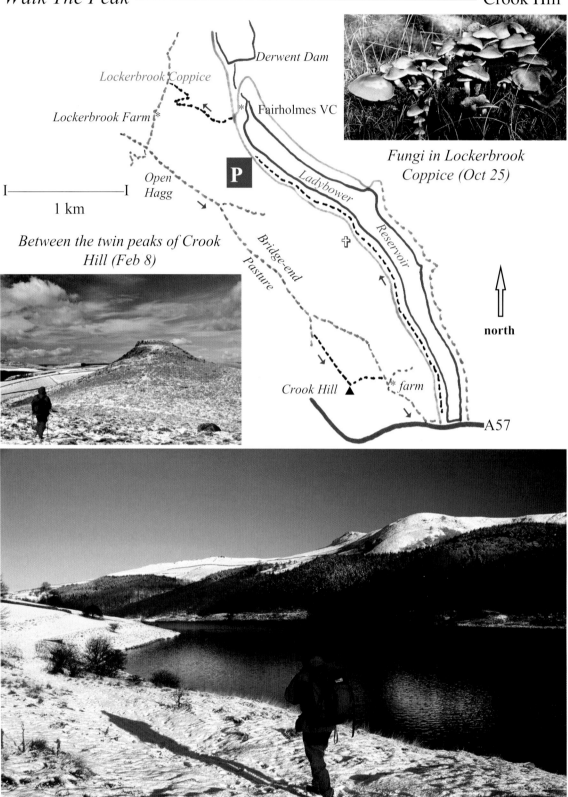

Lockerbrook Coppice

Derwent Dam

Lockerbrook Farm *

* Fairholmes VC

*Open
Hagg*

I————————I
1 km

*Fungi in Lockerbrook
Coppice (Oct 25)*

Ladybower

Reservoir

*Bridge-end
Pasture*

*Between the twin peaks of Crook
Hill (Feb 8)*

Crook Hill ▲

* *farm*

north

A57

Starting the waterside path, with Derwent Edge (Walk 16) above (Dec 31).

Route On the opposite side of the road to the entrance to **Fairholmes Visitor Centre** is a gate. Through this the path crosses a water channel and then winds up through **Lockerbrook Coppice**. There are also signs directing the way. Out of the woods the path crosses open ground to a track. Turn left along the track which leads down past **Lockerbrook Farm** Outdoor Centre on the left to a junction of four paths. Turn left on to a well-walked path which runs to the right of pine woods and across **Open Hagg**. After about a kilometre, avoid a path off to the left and continue across the rough grazing land of **Bridge-end Pasture** for another 1½ kms to another path junction. The twin summits of **Crook Hill** are now in view. Take the right fork, and over a stile the way is now clear for an ascent of the hills. Both are best approached from the left as you face them and both have pleasant, rocky perches. Descend left (east) off the highest summit and cross rough ground to a path. Turn right and soon you are directed left, through fields, to avoid a **farm** (Crookhill Farm). Cross the drive and paths lead down fields to a road, over which a gate leads to the waterside path beside **Ladybower Reservoir**. Turn left and the path leads all the way back to the lay-by (after about 2 kms the roadside war memorial can be visited).

Ashopton Viaduct and Bamford Edge from the waterside path (Oct 25)

19 Winhill Pike via Thornhill Carrs, Hope Cross and Ladybower

The natural fall at Yorkshire Bridge (April 24)

This ascent to one of the most popular viewpoints in The Peak avoids the tortuous slog up Parkin Clough. Instead, the way meanders up Thornhill Carrs, with ever expanding views, leaving just a short, steep ascent to the summit. On a clear day, the effort is rewarded with a fine panorama. An airy stroll (p.25) to Hope Cross is followed by a mossy woodland descent and a waterside track beside the western arm of Ladybower Reservoir.

Length 14 kms / 8.75 miles **Map** O/S Explorer OL1, *Dark Peak Area*, East Sheet
Start/Finish Heatherdene Car Park off the A6013, N of Bamford at SK 202 859
Terrain Well-defined tracks and paths, some may be muddy and slippery after rain
Refreshments None on route. *Yorkshire Bridge Inn* near CP. Other pubs, shop, Bamford
When To Go/What's There In late summer the flanks of Winhill Pike are heather-clad but each year sees less heather and more bracken, especially on the east side of the hill. Hope Cross has four destinations carved into its capping stone. The guide post was originally erected in 1737 at a junction of two packhorse ways to direct travellers off the old Roman Road and into the Hope Valley. When Ladybower Reservoir is full, a pair of spillage shafts near the headwall consume the overflow in an awesome and rather disturbing spectacle which can be seen from wall belvederes. There is a Millennium sculpture near Yorkshire Bridge, one of a number in the area. Buzzard and kestrel float above Hope Brink and the call of the curlew haunts the valley below in summer. From the reservoir shore, tufted duck, cormorant and heron can be seen angling for crustaceans and fish. The damp woods deliver mosses, lichens, liverworts, wood sorrel and dozens of fungi. In winter, goldcrests frequent the pines near Hope Cross. Dipper and grey wagtail inhabit the fall at Yorkshire Bridge and wild honeysuckle adorns Thornhill Carrs. **Nearby** at Bradwell is the spectacular Bagshaw Cavern. Adventure trips are occasionally arranged for novices: Mr Revell, 5 Main Road, Bradwell, Hope Valley (01433 620540).

Storm-light on Thornhill Carrs (Dec 12)

Approaching the trig pillar on Winhill Pike. In the distance, to the right of the walker are Lose Hill on The Great Ridge (Walk 21) and, beyond, Kinder Scout (Dec 31).

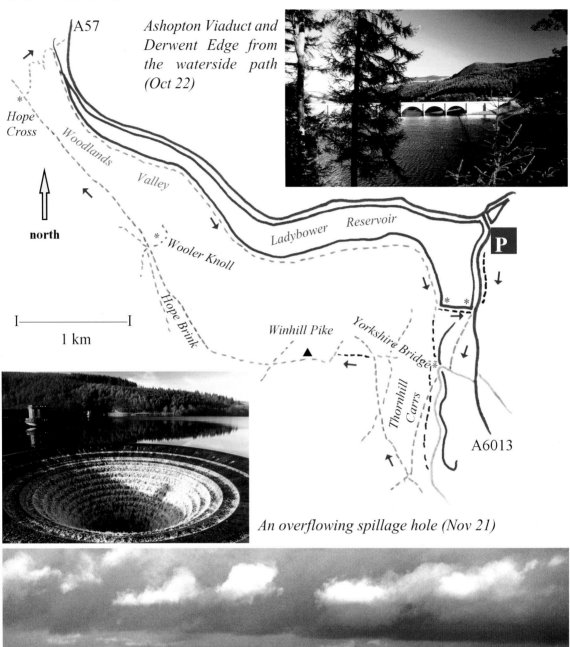

A57

Ashopton Viaduct and Derwent Edge from the waterside path (Oct 22)

Hope Cross

Woodlands

Valley

north

Wooler Knoll

Ladybower   Reservoir

P

Hope Brink

Winhill Pike

Yorkshire Bridge

Thornhill Carrs

A6013

I————————I
1 km

An overflowing spillage hole (Nov 21)

A winter storm looms over the rocky summit ridge of Winhill Pike (Dec 12)

Route Walk past the toilet block in the car park (noting the carved seat) and continue on the path that runs south and above the **A6013**. To the right, your objective, **Winhill Pike**, peeps above the forest. The path leads down to the A6013. Cross the road and take the footpath on the left (not the headwall path) which descends to a viewpoint with seats at the foot of the dam. Onwards, the path meanders to reach a gate at a minor road. (Before joining the road, it is now possible to follow the path upstream to the natural fall on the River Derwent). Turn right, through the gate and cross **Yorkshire Bridge**. Turn left, immediately cross the road and then turn right up either of two entrances to a path. Go up the path, cross a bridleway (once a railway line) and continue uphill through more hawthorn scrub and finally up wooden steps to a 4-way junction. You are now on **Thornhill Carrs**, and there are ever - expanding views. Turn right at the junction, go through a gate, and keep ahead at a path junction. The path, now level, runs right of a wall and arrives at another 4-way junction at the start of woodland. Here, turn left through conifers for a short distance before emerging from the trees at a wall stile. The way ahead is now obvious, as a path and steps lead uphill to the rocky summit-ridge of Winhill Pike and the trig pillar. Continue along the ridge and descend to a sandy path which runs west across the heather-clad Win Hill. Go ahead at a path junction. After about ½ km, the path swings right (north-west), along **Hope Brink** and meets another path junction after about 1 km. Here, walk ahead on the path leading to pines. Now, continue on the path that runs to the left of the pines for a couple of kms to reach **Hope Cross**, over the wall on the left. Here, turn right through a gate/door into woodland. Follow the path down through the damp, mossy woods. The path may occasionallly appear to fork, but all routes down lead to the wide track that runs along the western arm of **Ladybower Reservoir**. Turn right, and follow the track for almost 6 kms to the headwall of the reservoir. Turn left, walk across the wall and turn left on the roadside path which leads, with fine views, to the CP entrance across the A6013.

Crook Hill (Walk 18), from opposite Heatherdene car park entrance (Dec 31)

North Lees Hall, Bamford Edge and Stanage Edge

Stanage Edge and the chapel ruins were locations for "Pride & Prejudice" (July 9)

For years, climbers on Bamford Edge had the panorama of Ladybower and the Upper Derwent to themselves. Nowadays, the scene features in most publications on The Peak. As well as that scintillating view, this walk visits North Lees Hall; an ancient settlement; an idyllic picnic site beside a pond; and crosses the moors to ever-popular Stanage Edge.

Length 12 kms / 7.5 miles Map O/S Explorer OL1, *Dark Peak Area*, East Sheet
Start/Finish Hollin Bank car park (P&D) beneath Stanage Edge at SK 237 838
Terrain Paths and tracks over fields and moors. A little roadwork. 1½ kms are over heather moors and damp heath where there are no or only vestigial paths. Navigation is straightforward, however. Falls from the top of the edges could be fatal. A few inclines.
Refreshments None on route. Nearby Hathersage has shops, café and pubs.
When To Go/What's There If you go in April or May, be aware of ground nesting birds as you cross Bamford Moor. These include golden plover, snipe, curlew, whinchat and grouse. Mountain hares are on the moor, and you may be fortunate in summer to see short-eared owls rise lazily into the air if disturbed. Skylarks sing aloft, and you might glimpse a ring ouzel. Kestrels hover above. Foxglove, trefoil, harebell, cotton-grass, tormentil and hawkweeds flower. The pond supports brown hawker dragonflies and common blue damselflies. Sixteenth century North Lees Hall has romantic links to Charlotte Brontë's *Jane Eyre*. You could be lucky and arrive on an open day. Below and 100 metres past the trig pillar on High Neb, lie much-photographed millstones. Also from here, Minninglow may be seen 18 miles away almost due south. Numbered stone water basins are dotted along Stanage Edge. Finding these can help to motivate the kids as they tire near the end of the walk. Number 35 is near Stanage End, but if you breach the edge in a direct line from Bamford Moor (see Route), you will most likely find No 17 and walk on to No 1. There are settlement remains and, opposite, arched chapel ruins (photo).

Top Left. *The ancient pines above Hollin Bank car park (Oct 2).*

Top Right. *Approaching the entrance to North Lees Hall. The hall was originally the home of the Eyre family whose ancestry dates back to Norman times. Charlotte Brontë may have been inspired by North Lees to create* Jane Eyre's *Thornfield Hall.*

Left. *Climbers on Stanage Edge (Aug 23). Most now contribute to the Stanage Forum by avoiding the buttresses on which ring ouzels nest. Signs are put up near to the nest crags. Our walk across the top of the edge avoids the sensitive areas. Forum website : www.peakdistrict.org\stanage*

Bottom Left. *Rock basin No. 33 lies near Stanage End (Aug 23). It is written that the basins, with their grooved water-channels, were made to provide water for grouse. Odd, when natural water abounds.*

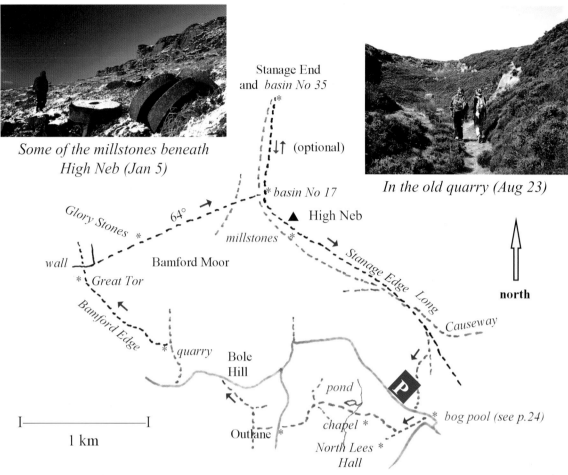

Some of the millstones beneath
High Neb (Jan 5)

In the old quarry (Aug 23)

Stanage End
and *basin No 35*
*

↓↑ (optional)

* *basin No 17*

▲ High Neb

64° ➚

Glory Stones *

millstones *

Stanage Edge Long

north

wall

Bamford Moor

* *Great Tor*

Causeway

Bamford Edge

←

* *quarry*

Bole
Hill

↓

P

I——————————I

1 km

pond

←

chapel *

←

* *bog pool (see p.24)*

Outlane *

*North Lees
Hall* *

On Stanage Edge in winter (Jan 5)

Route Turn left out of the car park. A path leads down left of the toilet block to another path. Turn right to a gate/stile. If you wish to visit **North Lees Hall**, walk down the left path for 200 metres or so, then return here. Take the path right which leads to a stile. Turn left over the stile and walk down through the boulder field with its ancient settlement remains to another stile. Cross the stream via the stepping stones and walk ahead up steps to the **pond**. The path onwards leads over fields and stiles and then between walls to Green's House. Keep straight on up the drive to **Outlane**. Cross the road and take the footpath opposite which leads to a stile. Go over, turn right and, near to the 2nd pylon in the field, turn right, up the field, to a wooden stile. Turn right over the stile and almost immediately left (signed *Bamford Road*). The path leads through woods to a minor road. Turn left and follow the road for about ½ km to a gate/stile on the right. This path leads uphill to a heather-clad old quarry. Walk to the end of the quarry and climb up to its rim. Here, take the 2nd path on the left which leads to a stone grouse butt. Turn left, down to the start of **Bamford Edge** and turn right to the viewpoint at Great Tor. Now descend the path a little more then turn right, off it, keeping just to the right of a dilapidated wall. From the corner of the wall (where it turns 90° left), walk ahead over the heather moor on a bearing of 64°. After about ½ km you should arrive at a rockfield, the **Glory Stones**. In view is a conspicuous line of stone fence-posts. Keep on the same heading, cross the wet heathland, and breach **Stanage Edge** at one of the gaps. If you plan to visit **Stanage End**, it will add a further 2 kms. Turn right at the top of the edge and walk past the trig pillar on **High Neb**. Later, and soon after basin No 1, **Long Causeway** reaches the edge. Follow it for about 100 metres then rejoin the path along the edge via a stile. About 300 metres later and, opposite a conspicuous eroded outcrop on the left, turn right down an ancient, worn path to the CP.

Ladybower Reservoir and the Upper Derwent from Great Tor, Bamford Edge (Nov 2)

21 The Great Ridge, Castleton, Cave Dale and The Winnats Pass

The Winnats Pass and Mam Tor from the path to the Winnats (Jan 29)

A tour of The Peak District - in one walk! An undulating ridge walk over the shale and grits of the "Shivering Mountain" to Lose Hill; then a descent to the village of Castleton, followed by a limestone dale and a spectacular craggy pass. Add four show caves, a hill fort, a castle, mine relics, a semi-precious gemstone and the tiered remains of a much repaired road swept away by endless landslips, and you have a special day out. Start early.

Length 15 kms / 9.4 miles **Map** O/S Explorer OL1, *Dark Peak Area*, East Sheet
Start/Finish Mam Nick car park, just outside Castleton on the A625 at SK 123 832
Terrain A long walk on well-walked paths and tracks. There is a loose, uphill pull up to Back Tor, which has to be taken with care. Parts of Cave Dale are stony underfoot.
Refreshments Pubs, cafés, shops and chips at Castleton, conveniently half way round.
When To Go/What's There Expansive views from The Great Ridge and Hurd Low. Mam Tor was a hill fort and bear and wolf bones have been found in Windy Knoll Cave. In Castleton, *The Gift Shop* has a fine array of Blue John (a beautiful form of fluorspar, unique to here). The Norman remains of Peveril Castle and a rope-making demonstration prior to the depths of the Peak Cavern may also tempt you into an extended lunch break. Garland Day on 29 May (Oak Apple Day), is a floral rite observed towards sunset, but sadly abused by some locals who plunder stands of wild flowers. The Treak Cliff Cavern boasts some preserved concretions; the other two show caves are poor value. We pass the Odin Mine and adjacent ore-crushing mill en route to part of the A625 that could grace a disaster movie. At Xmas, Castleton is well-lit. In summer, small heath butterfly, wheatear, and little owl may appear. Plants include mountain pansy, green spleenwort, hawkweeds, gorse and small-flowered cranesbill. *Titan*, now the deepest cave in the UK was realised after seven years hard work by local cavers and geophysics has offered a huge yet to date elusive cavern beneath the Winnats. **Nearby** Rushup Edge awaits, too.

Top Left. *After heavy snow, Mam Tor's 70 metre gully is used as practise for major climbs.* **Top Right.** *The Great Ridge from the summit of Lose Hill, also called Ward's Piece in honour of the landowner who donated it to the National Trust.* **Middle Left.** *Lower Cave Dale (May 27).* **Bottom.** *Mam Tor from near the end of the walk (Dec 29).*

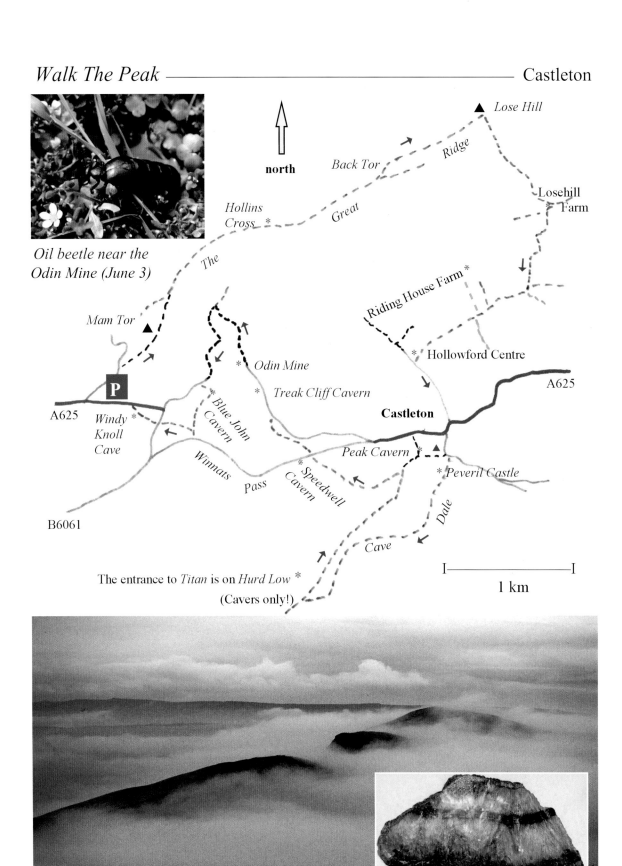

Oil beetle near the Odin Mine (June 3)

north

Lose Hill

Back Tor · · · Ridge

Hollins Cross *

Great

Losehill * Farm

The

Mam Tor

Riding House Farm *

P

Odin Mine *

Hollowford Centre *

Treak Cliff Cavern *

A625

Windy Knoll Cave *

Blue John Cavern *

Castleton

A625

Winnats

Pass

Speedwell Cavern *

Peak Cavern *

Peveril Castle *

B6061

Dale

The entrance to *Titan* is on *Hurd Low* *

Cave

(Cavers only!)

I—————————————I

1 km

The Great Ridge from Mam Tor (Jan 9). **Inset.** *The crystalline Blue John*

120

Route Walk to the top of the CP and take the steps up to the road. Go right, up the road and after about 50 metres take the gate on the right and the steps to the summit of **Mam Tor**. Turn right at the trig pillar and walk carefully down to grassy paths which run along the old fort walls to join the main path cresting **The Great Ridge**. There is a pillar at **Hollins Cross** and another airy kilometre leads to **Back Tor**. Just before the ascent, go over the stile on the left in a dip. Onwards leads up to the toposcope atop **Lose Hill** and one of the views of The Peak. Just below the summit a plaque commemorates G.H.B. Ward. Now turn right down the paving to a stile. Cross this to another stile ahead. Once over, turn 90° left, walk downhill, pass a finger post and go through the gate ahead at the rear of **Losehill Farm**. Then turn right through another gate (signed *Castleton*) to round the farm and join the farm drive. This doglegs down to Spring House Farm where you go through a gate and very soon turn right (signed to *Castleton*) down a lane. Turn left at a junction to the entrance/gate to **Riding House Farm**. Take the small gate to the left to stepping stones and cross a field to join a track. Turn left and keep left past **Hollowford Centre** to join the A625 at **Castleton**. Go right and then left up Castle Street (pub). At the top, turn left and then right into **Cave Dale**. This is followed gently uphill for about 2 kms until a path junction is reached. Here, bear sharp right, descend **Hurd Low** (views) to reach in a km a path T-junction at a wall. Turn left to meet the road at the bottom of the **Winnats Pass**. Cross, take the path ahead to join the road at the foot of the **Treak Cliff Cavern**. This is the relict stretch of the A625 and is followed uphill, past the **Odin Mine** on the left; the ore-crushing ring on the right and up and on all the road upheavals to a track on the left down to the **Blue John Cavern**. At the shop, bear right to the top of the Winnats road and views of the pass. Now backtrack a little and turn left on a path to the **B6061**. Cross, and a path ahead leads to **Windy Knoll**, with its natural cave shelter, the **A625** and the car park.

Peveril Castle from Cave Dale (May 27). The walker is now above the Peak Cavern.

<table>
<tr><td>**22**</td><td>**Mother Cap, Carl Wark, Higger Tor and The Burbage Edges**</td></tr>
</table>

An unusual low-arc rainbow over Higger Tor (centre) and Carl Wark (Oct 22)

This short walk through a justifiably popular area visits the isolated monolith of Mother Cap; the viewpoint at Over Owler Tor; the ancient fort of Carl Wark and the rugged plateau of Higger Tor, before returning via the crags and quarries of North and South Burbage. On route, there are a number of interesting natural and man-made phenomena.

Length 9 kms / 5.6 miles **Map** O/S Explorer OL 1, *Dark Peak Area*, East Sheet
Start/Finish Surprise Corner Car Park (P&D) off the A6187 at SK 252 801
Terrain Moorland paths, some of which can be tacky after rain. A few short inclines.
Refreshments None on route. Weekend vans at CPs; short detour to the *Fox House Inn*.
When To Go/What's There This walk for all seasons is most scenic when the heather is out or in winter when the moor grasses are golden and the bracken brown. On the way to *Mother Cap* is a stone resembling a turtle and an abandoned millstone (p.3). Further on, a "dolphin's head" rises from the boulders. A compass is carved on the crags of Over Owler Tor where, on summer Mondays, squirrels munch weekend picnic leftovers. The ancient *Earth Stone* lies beside a path near Higger Tor (photo). Carl Wark was originally thought to be an Iron Age fort, but archaeologists are now not so sure. The relict fort wall is impressive, and a worked boulder was possibly used for milling grain. But why didn't the settlers choose the higher and more defensively viable Higger Tor? The rocky outcrop opposite Fiddler's Elbow conceals a 15m roofed rift that appeals to the kids (in all of us). It is about half way up and along the rocks. Be careful, but have fun! On the descent from South Burbage lies an unfinished stone trough. Beneath it, on the lower path, is a circular trough. A few mountain hares have extended their range to Burbage Moor. Golden-ringed dragonflies, dippers and monkey-flower inhabit Burbage Brook and comma, red admiral and small heath butterflies flit in a gorse and heather channel near the car park.
Nearby on the A6187 is the *Toad's Mouth* rock or, as it possesses an eye, toad's head.

At Mother Cap (Jan 23). There is an easy(ish) way up round to the right.
Inset. *The ancient "Earth Stone" beside a path is worth the short detour. The cross within the orb symbol is of Christian origin, dating from the late 16th century after the earth had been "officially" accepted as being one of the planets (see sketch map).*

The Hope Valley and beyond from the flanks of Higger Tor (Oct 22)

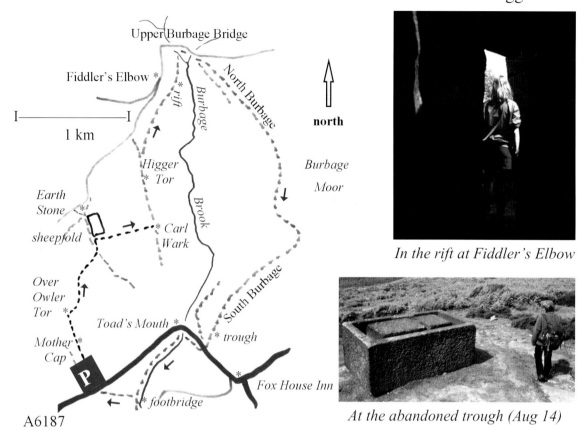

Upper Burbage Bridge

Fiddler's Elbow *

north

rift

Burbage

North Burbage

I————————I
1 km

*Higger
* Tor

*Burbage
Moor*

*Earth
Stone * *

sheepfold

Brook

* *Carl
Wark*

*Over
Owler
Tor * *

South Burbage

*Toad's Mouth *

* *trough*

*Mother * *
Cap*

P

* *
* *footbridge*

Fox House Inn

A6187

In the rift at Fiddler's Elbow

At the abandoned trough (Aug 14)

Carl Wark, Higger Tor and beyond from atop South Burbage Quarries (Jan 23)

Route Inside the car park, go through the gate opposite the entrance and walk uphill through silver birch trees to the millstone, turtle stone and then **Mother Cap**. Ahead, the path leads to **Over Owler Tor**, where a fine panorama is gained from the summit rocks. The path now swings right and descends through a pair of millstones before crossing moorland to the walled sheepfold. If you want to see the **Earth Stone**, keep to the left of the sheepfold and a path near the road ahead reveals it. However, our route turns right at the sheepfold and crosses damp heathland (engraved boulders on right) to **Carl Wark**, where an information board awaits. An obvious path leads left from the wall on the northern aspect of the fort and eventually rises to **Higger Tor**. Near the top, there are a number of various scrambles and ascents. At the top, on the left, are rocks with holes and views, but the route slants right across the plateau before descending. At a fork, keep to the right and follow the path north. As the path starts to rise again, rocks can be seen nearby on the right. These contain the **rift**, which is worth exploring. The path leads above these rocks and descends to cross two streams emanating from arches beneath **Upper Burbage Bridge**. After crossing the second stream, the path rises to meet another path coming in from the road on the left. Ahead is the start of **North Burbage** Rocks. Proceed along the path above the crags. After the end of the edge, the path undulates to X-paths where there is a needless cairn. Go ahead at this junction and the moorland path ultimately bears right and leads above the rocks and climbing quarries of **South Burbage**. As the path descends, it passes the abandoned stone **trough** and emerges at a gate on the **A6187**. (Here, you can either turn left to the **Fox House** or right to the **Toad's Mouth**). Whatever, cross the road, go through another gate and immediately turn right. Descend to a footbridge over **Burbage Brook**. Cross the footbridge and turn left. Follow the right bank of the brook for about ¾ km until another **footbridge** appears on the left. Opposite this, a path leads up to the right and leads through a pleasant, heather-clad shallow gulley to the A6187 and the car park.

On the path through the heather from Over Owler Tor to Higger Tor (Sept 12)

23 Old Clough, Abney Moor and Offerton Edge

The rustic wooden stile on the way to Callow Wood (Jan 6)

This figure-of-eight trip starts with a walk beside the River Derwent to stepping stones across the river. The route doesn't cross the stones but, if the river is low, who wouldn't be tempted? As height is gradually gained from Offerton Hall, a spectacular vista of landmarks come in to view. Abney Moor leads to Offerton Edge and a woodland descent.

Length 14 kms / 8.75 miles **Map** O/S Explorer OL 1, *Dark Peak Area*, East Sheet
Start/Finish Car Park beside the outdoor swimming pool at Hathersage, off the B6001 (pay/display). There are a number of other car parks (inc railway station) and side roads.
Terrain Tracks and paths across moors and fields - some may be muddy. Some roads.
Refreshments Pubs, cafes, shops at Hathersage. *Plough Inn* near Leadmill Bridge.
When To Go/What's There A walk for all seasons, with an abundance of fine views. Tufted duck, dipper, little grebe and grey wagtail ply the waters of The Derwent. Goosanders, too, were becoming frequent, but they are being shot as they are deemed too predatory on trout. Fancy having the cheek fishing to live, whilst others fish for fun! Was the stone near the TV mast, engraved 1666 with fading initials, a personal memorial to a loved one lost to the plague? And why (at the time of writing) does the BBC Shatton Edge relay station need eight locks on the gate? The Siney Sitch area supports snipe, curlew, water boatman, common hawker and black darter dragonflies, and plants such as marsh pennywort, bell heather, sundew, bog pondweed, cross-leaved heath and bog asphodel. Foxgloves, liverworts and "fairy-cup" lichens are beside the path to Old Clough. Kestrel, merlin and hobby are among visiting raptors. Small copper and small heath butterflies flit past the tumuli on the heather moors. If you return sweating after a summer outing, why not join other masochists in the alfresco pool? **Nearby** The Derbyshire and Lancashire Gliding Club at Camphill has a viewing "car park" (SK 182 785) and also offers tuition and one-off flights in two-seater craft (01298 871 270).

Crossing the stepping stones over the River Derwent (July 29)

Hathersage from Offerton Edge (Feb 14). Stanage Edge is on the skyline.

Leftovers for sheep on Abney Moor

Glider preparing for take-off from Camphill

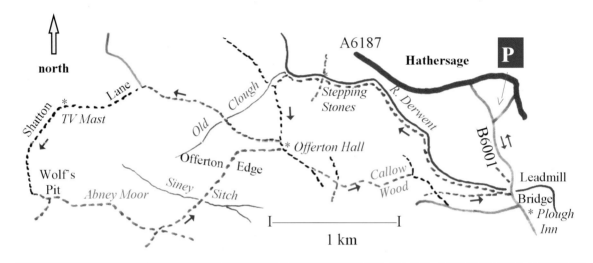

Where the path from Old Clough reaches Shatton Lane (Jan 6)

Route From the car park walk down Oddfellows Road to the **B6001**. Turn left and walk down the road for about ½ km to **Leadmill Bridge**. Cross the bridge and turn right through the stile and gate onto the path that runs beside the **River Derwent**. The riverside path soon enters Goose Nest Wood, crosses two footbridges and leads through successive gates until it reaches the **Stepping Stones** across the Derwent. After a play on the stones, continue upstream on the left bank and up steps on the path that then falls to a footbridge. Cross, and soon turn left up a track to a gate with stile. Turn left and immediately right up a lane which leads to the fine hamlet of Offerton. The lane snakes uphill past the entrance to **Offerton Hall** on the left. Shortly after, at a left bend, turn 1st right off the track at a gate with stile onto a bridleway, which pleasantly leads to **Old Clough** and subsequently **Shatton Lane**. Go through the gate or over the ladder stile, turn left and follow the track uphill to the **TV Mast**. The 1666 stone is about 300m past the mast beside a gate on the left. Further on, bear left (signed *Abney & Brough*) on the track churned up by 4x4s, then, mercifully, soon after, turn left off the track at **Wolf's Pit** on to a path signed *Highlow* and *Stoke Ford*. This grassy path leads to a stile and meanders downhill for about 1 km through the heather of **Abney Moor** to X-paths (not signed). Take the left fork, cross the moor to **Siney Sitch** and **Offerton Edge**, where the path descends to the track to Offerton Hall. Turn right, and after about 250m, turn left off the track and over a stile on to a path which leads to the rustic stile (photo) and, via a stile, to a farmyard. Go through the left gate, down the field, enter and walk down through **Callow Wood**. Fields then lead to a gate at a track. Turn right, uphill and when at the entrances to Broadhay and Mount Pleasant Farms, go left (gate) down fields (wall stile) to the waterside path and the B6001.

Crossing Siney Sitch (Feb 14)

Walks On White Peak Map ——————— West Sheet

(Explorer Outdoor Leisure Series No 24)

Approaching Parkhouse Hill from Hollinsclough with High Wheeldon, the final summit on the walk, the furthest right (Walk 28, Dec 29)

Combs Edge, Castle Naze and Fernilee Reservoir

Fernilee Reservoir from the headwall road of Errwood Reservoir (Sept 21)

This fairly tough outing rises from the scenic but popular Goyt Valley to an airy traverse of Combs Edge before descending placidly to the village of Combs. A rugged ascent to Wythen Lache precedes a wild descent to Fernilee Reservoir, which is followed home.

Length 16 kms / 10 miles **Map** O/S Explorer OL24, *White Peak Area*, West Sheet
Start/Finish Lay-by CP with conveniences at the bottom of Goyt's Lane at SK 018 758
Terrain A mixture of easy tracks; uphill and downhill paths over rough farm pasture and above crags, some of which may be soggy; and some roadwork. Horses may be encountered in some fields to negotiate, especially near Thorny Lee and Overhill Farms.
Refreshments The *Beehive Inn* at Combs also serves food.
When To Go/What's There A wild, rustic walk for all seasons, but in winter be prepared for some very cold winds sweeping over Combs Edge! There is a continental-style shrine beside Goyt's Lane if you approach the car park from the A5004. As you crest the rise towards White Hall, the view ahead includes Chinley Churn; South Head and Mount Famine (Walk 12) and Kinder Scout beyond. The heather, cross-leaved heath and purple moor-grass from Combs Moss encroach to the crags of Combs Edge as do the associated red grouse and meadow pipit. Below the edge is a different landscape, with rough pasture, bracken and soft-rush. In summer, skylark and curlew call and you may see a ring ouzel near the crags of Castle Naze, but more likely rock climbers. Here, a stile allows access to the Iron Age hill fort, where you can view the banks built to supplement the natural defences. On the road below is an ancient parish boundary post. You may flush snipe from wetlands, and cormorant, goosander and widgeon may visit Fernilee Reservoir. Waterside residents include squirrel, bullfinch, goldcrest and long-tailed tit.
Nearby For another Goyt walk try Pym Chair (P at SJ 994 767) to Windgather Rocks; descend to Midshires Way; follow it south to The Street; walk back uphill to Pym Chair.

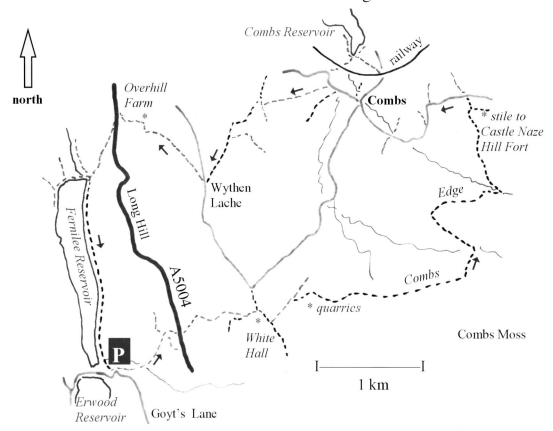

north

Combs Reservoir

railway

Overhill Farm

*

Long Hill

A5004

Fernilee Reservoir

Wythen Lache

Combs

* stile to Castle Naze Hill Fort

Edge

Combs

* quarries

*

White Hall

Combs Moss

P

Erwood Reservoir

Goyt's Lane

I———————I

1 km

The isolated Jenkin Chapel (an amalgam of house and chapel) is near the start of this walk and also Walk 25 (Dec 12). **Inset.** *The continental shrine beside Goyt's Lane.*

Route Go through the gate in the car park (sign to **Long Hill**), walk down through the woods and cross the footbridge. The path now rises steeply (with expanding views behind) to eventually join a track which leads, right, to the **A5004**. Over the road, the path rises again before meandering down to join a track to **White Hall** Outdoor Pursuits Centre. Stay on this track (avoid lane on left) and remain on it as it rounds the centre on the right. As the track rises, avoid a stile on the left and continue uphill for about 150 metres to a stile and footpath on the left signed to *Combs*. Walk down the rough field (wall on right) to a stile which leads you to the other side of the wall. About 200 metres down the path forks. Turn right and the path rounds **quarry** spoil mounds, crosses stiles and walls and then pleasantly rises to **Combs Edge**. Keep ahead and follow the narrow path along the edge for about 3 kms. At the end of the edge, and before the stile to **Castle Naze Hill Fort**, follow the well-worn path ahead down the grassy slope to a minor road. Turn left down the road and follow it to and through the village of **Combs** to the *Beehive Inn*. Take the road to the left of the inn, pass a lane leading off left and, about 70 metres past, turn left up the track with footpath sign and cattle grid. The track reaches farm buildings on the left and, after a gate, leave the track on a path to the right and to the left of a hedge. More gates and stiles, some awkward, lead ahead to a gate and walled path beside a farm on the right. Follow the drive uphill. It bends to the right and soon a track leads sharp left at a gate. Follow the track to a minor road. Turn right, cross the road and go over the wall stile. The path slants right, across rough, airy land (avoid minor left forks) for about ½ km to reach a wooden stile in a wall corner to the left of a small plantation. Go over the stile, and then another ahead leads to the drive to **Overhill Farm**. Here, turn right into the farmyard where a wall stile is on the left. Follow the field straight down to a gate. Turn right to the A5004 again. Cross, turn left on the footpath and, after about 100 metres, go down the wide track on the right. This leads to **Fernilee Reservoir**. Follow the left waterside path to the CP.

On the path back beside Fernilee Reservoir (Sept 21)

Looking out to Combs Reservoir and beyond from Castle Naze Rocks (Aug 28)

Castle Naze from about half way along Combs Edge (Aug 28)

25 Errwood Reservoir, Shining Tor and Goyt's Moss

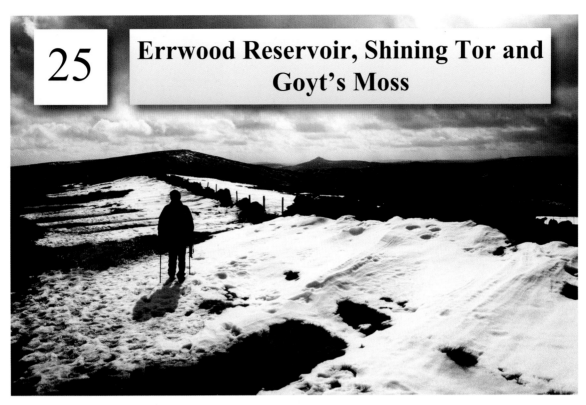

Across The Tors, with pyramidal Shutlingsloe (Walk 27) in the distance (March 10)

This walk encompasses the variety of the lovely Goyt Valley, with its reservoirs, moors and ridges. From the ruins of Errwood Hall the walk ascends to Pym Chair for an airy trek to Shining Tor, then descends to Errwood Reservoir and, optionally, Goyt's Moss.

Length 16 kms / 10 miles **Map** O/S Explorer OL24, *White Peak Area*, West Sheet
Start/Finish Errwood Hall Car Park on the Errwood to Derbyshire Bridge minor road at SK 012 748. This road is closed on some Bank Holidays and many Sundays. If you must go then, there are three alternative car parks on the route (see O/S map).
Terrain A toughish undulating walk on paths and tracks over rough ground and moors. There will be boggy sections after prolonged rainfall or snowmelt on the moorland paths.
Refreshments None, other than summer ice cream vans at some car parks.
When To Go/What's There A fine walk for all seasons, but if the westerlies are in full flight, be prepared for a good buffeting along The Tors. In May and early June the azaleas and rhododendrons (especially near the ruins of Errwood Hall) are a fine sight. The larches and grasses in autumn turn yellow and gold. Some bogs support lousewort. Snipe may arise startled from flushes; woodcock are in the hall hinterland; red grouse on the moors and skylarks sing above the heathery Tors. In summer, ring ouzels are regular visitors. An occasional juvenile osprey may be spotted on passage at Errwood Reservoir. If you're fortunate (and quiet), red deer can be observed, notably from where the path from Shooter's Clough meets the descent path, and from the path to the shrine. The hall was the home of the Grimshawe family, whose graves are in the woods above. They can be seen on the left as you descend to the reservoir. The family built a shrine to their beloved governess, Dolores de Bergrin, which is worth a reverent peek inside en route.
Nearby is the Jenkin Chapel (SJ 984 765, photo p.132) and, for a mystery from 1755, read the roadside memorial to John Turner at SJ 977 759, but don't park beside the stone.

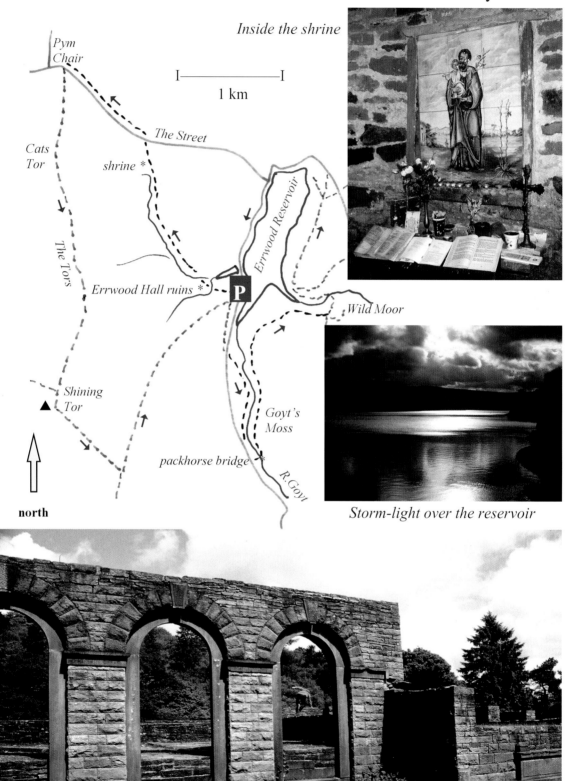

Inside the shrine

1 km

Pym
Chair

The Street

Cats
Tor

shrine *

The Tors

Errwood Reservoir

Errwood Hall ruins *

P

Wild Moor

Shining
Tor

Goyt's
Moss

packhorse bridge *

R.Goyt

north

Storm-light over the reservoir

Some of the ruins of Errwood Hall (Aug 7)

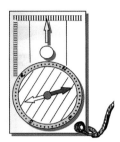

Route Walk uphill from the information board to a wall. Go through the narrow, right entrance and metal gate. The path leads on through damp, mossy woodland to the signpost (right) to **Errwood Hall**. From the ruins, a path leads down to, and crosses a stream to a junction. Turn right, up steps, then left, signed to *The Shrine*. The path rises steadily uphill; passes through ancient pines to the circular, stone **shrine** (path down, steps back up) and on to a road (**The Street**). Turn left, uphill, making use of the path up the right verge. Shortly after a stile on the right (to *Windgather*), carefully cross the road (blind summit), and take the path signed to *Shining Tor*. This leads to **Cats Tor**, where pyramidal Shutlingsloe rises ahead; Combs Edge to the east and White Nancy (p.241) to the west. Onwards, **The Tors** fall and eventually rise to the ladder stile and trig pillar at **Shining Tor**. Here, turn left (worryingly signed to the *Cat and Fiddle*) and on to a path junction through a gate. Turn left (signed *Errwood*). The path descends; passes the entrance to *Shooter's Clough* on the left; goes through a gate (Grimshawe graves, left) and falls to signed X-paths just above **Errwood Reservoir**. If you wish to shorten the walk here (by 5 kms), walk ahead to the CP. To continue, go right (*Goytsclough*) to a road. Cross, and take the track which leads down through woods to the **River Goyt**. A path then follows the river before rising to the road again. Turn left, and follow the road then path down to the **packhorse bridge**. Cross, and turn left on the path which leads over **Goyt's Moss**. The path crosses the moor and then bears right, to arrive at a metal bridge over a stream. Turn left over the bridge and the way ahead leads above the eastern shore of Errwood Reservoir, across fields and through a little woodland, to reach a road. Turn left, pass a CP with conveniences on the right, and follow the road as it doglegs to cross the headwall of the reservoir. Turn left at the road junction. Soon there is a path on the right verge and, ahead, the car park.

Approaching Errwood Reservoir before turning right to the packhorse bridge (Sept 29)

On the way down to Errwood Reservoir from Shining Tor (Nov 4)

We're not the only ones to cross the River Goyt by the packhorse bridge (Aug 7).
Goyt Bridge was salvaged when Fernilee and Errwood Reservoirs were constructed.

26 Chee Dale Gorge, Chee Tor and Blackwell

Looking down on Blackwell Cottages from near the end of the walk (July 16)

Chee Dale is by far the most spectacular gorge in The Peak and, for those familiar with France, not unlike a mini Verdon Gorge. This short walk has the bonus of unusual aerial views of the River Wye snaking its way through the limestone crags. Our route follows the river throughout its journey through the gorge, and then gains height for the views.

Length 7 kms / 4.4 miles **Map** O/S Explorer OL 24, *White Peak Area*, West Sheet
Start/Finish Lay-by on the A6 between Buxton and Taddington at SK 112 724
Terrain There are rocky terraces and stepping-stones which may be slippery/icy. Some paths may be muddy or indistinct. Take care if you choose to explore the top of the crags.
Refreshments Frequent mobile café at the lay-by. Beech Croft camp shop at Blackwell.
When To Go/What's There In winter, the damper crags in the gorge occasionally have cascades of icicles and the dippers are easier to approach. A heron or (rarely) a kingfisher may pass by at the start of the gorge. Grey wagtails are frequent. Scarlet elf cup and other fungi, together with lichens, mosses and ferns, drape moist areas of the ash, wych elm and hazel scrub, which supports many flowers and insects, including the rhinoceros beetle. Much of this area is a Derbyshire Wildlife Trust reserve and the gorge has been awarded cSAC status - the highest European classification. Saw-wort and orchids colonise the land disturbed by Romano-Britains above Chee Tor. Springs near the end of the gorge support monkey-flower and watercress. The crags are gems, with ten species of butterfly including common blue and dark green fritillary amongst the thyme, rockrose, knapweed, cowslip, bloody cranes-bill, globeflower, harebell, umbellifers, red campion, violet, hawkweeds, ox-eye daisy, corn salad, marjoram, scabious and kidney vetch which, in The Peak, is the food plant of the rare small blue butterfly. Other interesting plants include Nottingham catchfly, twayblade and fragrant orchid. Climbers perform on the crags. **Nearby** Monk's Dale, Peter Dale and Hay Dale are floral joys, too. Go in June.

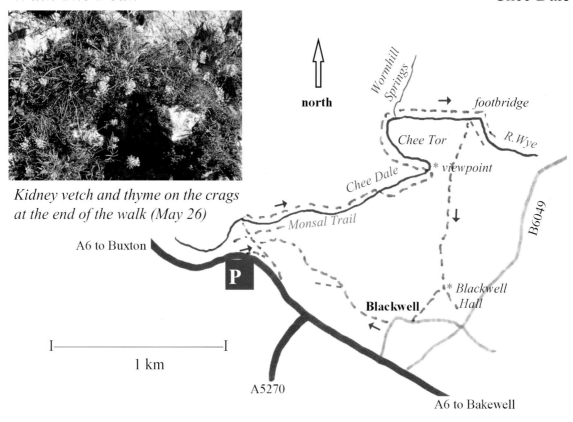

Kidney vetch and thyme on the crags at the end of the walk (May 26)

Looking down on The Monsal Trail from near the end of the walk (Aug 16)

Route From the lay-by, take the path which slants to the right and joins another path leading left, down the valley. Pass the path on the right to Blackwell (your return route), cross the **Monsal Trail** either by the bridge or the wall stiles and descend to the **River Wye** at a row of cottages. Cross the footbridge, turn right and follow the left bank of the Wye downstream. Soon, keep right at a path junction and then keep left at a footbridge (which rises to the **Monsal Trail** - never join the Monsal Trail). In high summer, early stretches of the riverside path may be overgrown with butterbur and meadow-sweet. As you pass through the gorge, you will encounter two sets of stepping stones and two footbridges. A further footbridge and plank are crossed over a stream at the end of the gorge and, about 300 metres on, a substantial, metal-railed **footbridge** spans the Wye. Cross and take the right fork up to an old wall. Now the indistinct path slants sharp left before wandering uphill to a finger post. Here, it is possible to walk 90° right for an aerial view of **Chee Dale** (p.142). Return, and follow the path through a stile and then a large field, where it hugs a wall on the right and meets a track to **Blackwell Hall**. Here, a signpost leads you right to a wall stile and through fields and more wall stiles to **Blackwell**. Turn right on the road and leave it after about 150 metres down a track on the right (signed *Pennine Bridleway, Chee Dale*). Go through the gate and later two more. The track now forks so leave the PB and take the right fork downhill for about 50 m to another gate on the left. Go through and angle right across the field to a wall stile near the bottom of the field. Another short field then leads to the top of the crags. The way back follows the path left, but a careful walkabout reveals some fine views. The path becomes rocky and stony as it spirals down (through a floral wonderland in mid-July) to the valley path, where you turn left, uphill, to the lay-by.

The River Wye in Chee Dale (May 26)

The first set of stepping stones leads through an atmospheric cleft (May 26). Do not attempt this walk after prolonged rainfall, as the steps and path may be flooded.

Looking down on walkers entering Chee Dale Tunnel on the Monsal Trail from the viewpoint (May 26). A quiet few minutes may reveal weasels from the nearby walls.

27 Shutlingsloe, Wildboarclough and Three Shire Heads

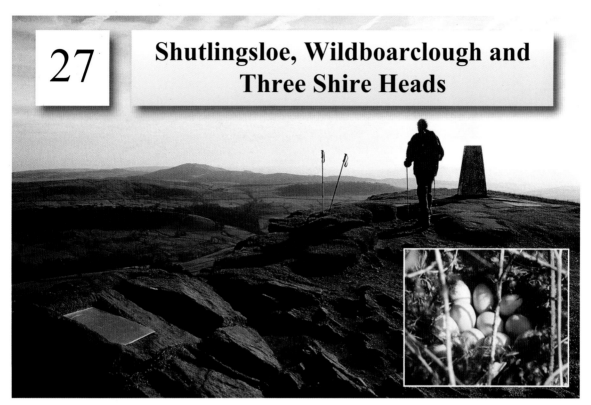

At the summit of Shutlingsloe (Feb 11). **Inset.** *Mallard's nest beside Clough Brook.*

This fairly tough walk through a rugged landscape starts with an ascent of the isolated crown of Shutlingsloe; passes through sleepy Wildboarclough en route to popular Three Shire Heads; rises to the River Dane watershed and Danebower Hollow for a panoramic view, before tumbling down beside Cumberland Brook for a welcome downhill home run.

Length 12.5 kms / 7.8 miles **Map** O/S Explorer OL 24, *White Peak Area*, West Sheet
Start/Finish Clough House Car Park about 1km north of Wildboarclough at SJ 987 698
Terrain A little roadwork is the respite from paths and tracks that for some reason all seem to be either stony, boggy or uphill. The final grovel up Shutlingsloe sure is uphill!
Refreshments None on route. Short (200m) detour to *Crag Inn* at Wildboarclough.
When To Go/What's There An exhilarating walk at any time of the year, but under snow the route may be hard to follow in places. The Cheshire Plain and the radio telescope dish of Jodrell Bank can be seen from the summit of Shutlingsloe, but the most expansive view en route rises from the path up and over Danebower Hollow. As befits a wild walk on grits, the wildlife is there, but in small numbers. Buzzard and kestrel are in the skies; curlew and meadow pipit on the moors and the odd dipper and grey wagtail on the River Dane. Brown hare and lapwing flit through farmland and rabbits excavate Cutthorn. Small copper and small heath butterflies flutter over rough pasture and speckled wood spiral together in the pleasant grounds of the church of St. Saviour, where a leaflet detailing the hamlet's industrial past may be purchased. The Old Post Office seems a rather large building in such a remote setting. There is a plaque to the floods of 1989. Rove beetles scuttle over sandy paths, and plants include soft rush, tormentil, common cotton-grass, great willowherb, hawkweeds, foxgloves, gorse, bilberry and heather.
Nearby 2 kms SW off the A54 is Blaze Farm with basic nature trail, tea rooms and, *Hilly Billy* home-made ice cream! NW, Trentabank Reservoir has viewpoints to its heronry.

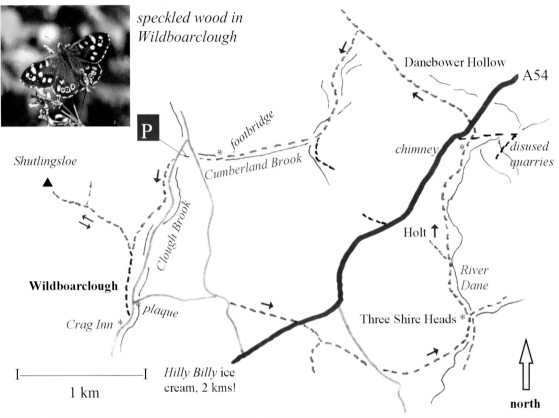

speckled wood in Wildboarclough

P

Shutlingsloe ▲

Wildboarclough

Crag Inn * * *plaque*

Clough Brook

footbridge

Cumberland Brook

Danebower Hollow

A54

chimney * *disused quarries*

Holt ↑

River Dane

Three Shire Heads *

I————————I
1 km

Hilly Billy ice cream, 2 kms!

north

Shutlingsloe emerging from the mist (Sept 21). Note how trekking poles stop the walker from falling over!

Route Turn left out of the car park. After a couple of hundred metres go over the stile on the right hand side of the road. Follow the path through more gates and stiles; pass a barn on the left and a dwelling on the right and continue on the track to a cattle grid and gates. Turn right before the grid and walk up the metalled farm track. Leave the track at the entrance gates to the farm and walk uphill through fields and stiles to the summit of **Shutlingsloe**, ignoring a waymark sign pointing right at a stile. From the summit, retrace your steps to the cattle grid, go through a gate and walk down the track to a road. Turn left then right, over **Clough Brook** (memorial plaque) and walk up the road, passing St Saviour's church and the Old Post Office at **Wildboarclough**. A road joins from the left and, soon after, leave the road at a right hand bend. Go up the track to a gate and follow the path ahead uphill and over rough and sometimes wet ground (boarding) to a road, the **A54**. Cross, and follow the path across the moor (sign to *Turn Edge*) to a minor road. Cross, and follow the stony track down to the waterfalls and packhorse bridge at **Three Shire Heads**. From here, continue on the track to the left of the bridge, bear right(ish) over stile/gate and follow the track beside the fledgling **River Dane**. Go right over the stile at a bridleway junction (to **Holt**) and enter a series of boggy areas, where the path is not too clear, but forge ahead to reach another stile, beside the river again. Go over, and a better path leaves The Dane to reach a ruin on the left. Head uphill to a chimney and beyond, a track. Cross, and climb the short, steep path ahead to the A54 again. Go through the gate over the road and follow the path up **Danebower Hollow** for about 1 km to a metal footpath sign. Turn left and follow the path down the moor to the rocky start of **Cumberland Brook**, which is crossed a few times before reaching a track junction. Go through the gate/stile ahead and follow the way down; over a stile then footbridge to a road and down to the car park.

Sheep drinking from the River Dane at Three Shire Heads (Sept 21)

Top. *Shutlingsloe from the duckboards near the A54 (Jan 7).* **Bottom.** *A similar view without the snow (Feb 11).* **Inset.** *The plaque on the bridge over Clough Brook commemorates the floods of 1989, when a seven metre wall of water swept down the valley destroying all the bridges and thus marooning the inhabitants of Wildboarclough.*

28 | Chrome Hill, Parkhouse Hill, Hollinsclough and High Wheeldon

Approaching Parkhouse Hill (left) and Chrome Hill from Earl Sterndale (May 11)

A tour of the ridges and spines of the reef limestone hills of the Upper Dove Valley. Just a few metres from the car the peaks come into view - and the adrenalin rises. This spectacular scenery was overlooked by walkers for many years but is now more popular. When clothed in snow, the area resembles a mini alpine landscape and, under these conditions, it is hard to believe that we are gazing over what was once a coral reef in a tropical sea. Coral limestone is hard to erode, which is why these peaks remain today.

Length 12 kms / 7.5 miles **Map** O/S Explorer OL 24, *White Peak Area*, West Sheet
Start/Finish Earl Sterndale, park on the side road adjacent to the church (SK 090 670)
Terrain Some steep ascents and, if you keep to all the crests of the ridges, there are a few airy steps - but these can all be avoided by paths a couple of metres below. The majority of the walk is on well-defined paths and tracks, so don't miss out on this classic.
Refreshments The *Quiet Woman* pub in Earl Sterndale - don't be deterred by the sign!
When To Go/What's There Although it is the marvellous scenery that most catches the eye, the tree that has almost devoured the commemorative stone opposite the pub is quaint, and less common flowers include orpine, maiden pink, gentian and, on some non-grazed ledges, Jacob's ladder. Hare, weasel, fox, whinchat, buzzard, lapwing, skylark and wheatear may appear. Chrome Hill has reef fossils on the descent outcrops and two ponds passed en route to Fough support frogs, newts, whirligig beetles, pondweeds, dragonflies and damselflies. **Nearby** Washgate Bridge at SK 052 674 is a charming packhorse bridge. The gravestone of William Billinge in Longnor churchyard is worth reading for his military exploits well into old age (he died aged 112 "just 150 yards from where he was born") and the village market hall (now a café/craft shop) still displays a tariff of the ancient tolls above the entrance. This small, rugged village still has four surviving pubs. SE of the village are surviving medieval strip fields and the "restored" Knowsley Cross.

147

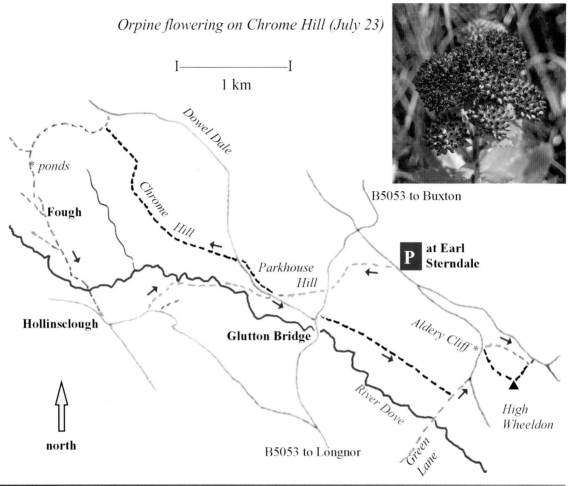

Orpine flowering on Chrome Hill (July 23)

I————————I
1 km

Dowel Dale

*ponds

Fough

Chrome Hill

B5053 to Buxton

P at Earl
Sterndale

*Parkhouse
Hill*

Hollinsclough

Aldery Cliff *

Glutton Bridge

River Dove

↑

north

Green Lane

B5053 to Longnor

*High
Wheeldon*

Looking back to Parkhouse Hill from the lower crest of the Chrome Hill ridge (Dec 29)

Route Face the pub and turn right, down the road and, after about 100 metres, take the narrow stile at a gate on the left. The track leads to stiles and paths that drop down to the **B5053**. Over the road the way leads to **Parkhouse Hill**, which can be ascended over access land once the walls end. Return to the path and continue to a cattle grid. Here, turn left up the concessionary path to **Chrome Hill** and bear immediately right to gain the ridge, which is followed (stile halfway) to the rocky summit. Descend the undulating ridge ahead, slant left at the bottom, and go right, over the stile. The path soon turns right, uphill, and then left to meet a farm track. Cross, and proceed ahead on an indistinct path over fields to meet the track to **Fough** (later signposted). From Fough, the path falls to cross the **River Dove** (footbridge) and rises to the hamlet of **Hollinsclough**. Turn left at the road, pass the old school, and take the first track on the left, which again crosses The Dove, to meet a minor road. Turn right to **Glutton Bridge** (phone box), then left for a few metres on the **B5053** before taking the track opposite. This leads through gates to **Green Lane**. Bear left at this T-junction and join a minor road which soon passes the rock-climbing face beneath **Aldery Cliff**. Go over the stile on the right (NT sign) and walk uphill to meet a prominent path coming in from the left. Here, turn right up the grassy steps to the summit pillar atop **High Wheeldon**. Read the commemoration and bear right, down the airy north-west ridge, which passes the (sadly) gated entrance to Fox Hole Cave on the right, where ancient animal and human remains were excavated. Now continue to descend, with care, to the stile at the road again. Turn right and follow the road uphill to **Earl Sterndale**.

High Wheeldon from above Earl Sterndale (June 10)

At the bottom of the ridge up Chrome Hill. Two other couples, seen as dots, are approaching the summit (Dec 29).

Looking back to the bulk of Chrome Hill from the north (Aug 10). The undulating ridge down from the summit is often referred to in publications as "The Dragon's Back" but, in fairness, this title is probably a bit of an insult to The Andes.

29 Dane Valley, Hanging Stone, Lud's Church and Gradbach Hill

Approaching the pinnacle on Gradbach Hill (Aug 15)

This short and not too taxing walk packs in a number of fine views and interesting natural features. It starts through mossy woodland beside the River Dane; rises to the Hanging Stone and viewpoints; descends to the natural chasm of Lud's Church; a fording of Black Brook and an enchanting ancient lane leading to the viewpoints on wild Gradbach Hill.

Length 10 kms/6.25 miles **Map** O/S Explorer OL 24, *White Peak Area*, West Sheet
Start/Finish Gradbach Car Park, just before the signposted youth hostel at SJ 998 662
Terrain Stony paths and tracks and peaty paths over the moors. A little uphill work.
Refreshments None on route. Cold drinks fish farm; *Ship Inn*, Wincle (closed Mondays)
When To Go/What's There A walk for all seasons, with the damp woods dripping with mosses, lichens, wood sorrel, fungi and liverworts. Woodpecker, treecreeper, goldcrest, wren and nuthatch are in there, too. Heather carpets the high moors, and if bilberry-picking whets your appetite, then a rocky knoll provides a lunchtime treat. Dipper and grey wagtail are on the River Dane and very ancient larch, Scots pine, silver birch and beech trees are met. The deep, moss-cloaked rift of Lud's Church hosts many plant specialities, including oak fern. The Hanging Stone alludes to its overhanging stance, rather than more sinister overtones. It does, however, have two interesting plaques inset high into the grit and, from the top, The Roaches, Hen Cloud, Tittesworth Reservoir, Shutlingsloe and Sutton Common mast are in view. A short, medieval lane of foxgloves leads to Gradbach Hill, formerly via concession, but now on access land. There are fine views from the top of the heather-clad crags. If you are "in to fish", a ½ km extension to the Danesbridge Fish Company has catch-your-own and feed-the-fish opportunities. Act out science to get that trout home before it festers! **Nearby** SE of Leek, Froghall Wharf offers narrowboat trips (SK 026 476, *Explorer* 259) and, to make a day of it, you could devise a walk via a ride on the Churnet Valley Railway from Froghall Bridge Station.

Left. *Memorial to a faithful mastiff on the Hanging Stone. One of two plaques.*

Right. *Passing the standing stone (Jan 25).*

BENEATH THIS ROCK
AUGUST 1874 WAS BURIED
BURKE
A NOBLE MASTIFF
BLACK AND TAN.
FAITHFUL AS WOMAN
BRAVER THAN MAN.
A GUN AND A RAMBLE
HIS HEART'S DESIRE
WITH THE FRIEND OF HIS LIFE
THE SWYTHAMLEY SQUIRE

north

Valley

River Dane

Dane

rocky knoll *

FB

P

Gradbach

Ship Inn

Hanging Stone *

Lud's Church

ford

* Gradbach Hill

* standing stone

Black Brook

Danebridge

I————————I

1 km

fish farm

Approaching the Hanging Stone (Jan 25)

Route Turn right out of the car park and follow the lane to Gradbach Mill Youth Hostel. Continue up to a gate and a footpath. After about 80 metres, turn right through a stile then left along the path, which soon becomes a track. Leave the track where it turns sharp left and go through the wall stile. Walk down, cross the **footbridge** and rise to signposts beneath a wonderful beech tree. Turn right on the path to *Danebridge*, which soon follows close to the **River Dane** as it purls downstream at the foot of larch woods. The woods are followed by open fields, well waymarked, to another short section of woodland and then to a gate/stile just before **Danebridge** itself. About 50 metres beyond the gate, turn left up the concession path, signed to the **Hanging Stone**. (If you wish to visit the fish farm, walk on to the bridge, turn right over it, and then left to fish). The concession path leads up through mossy woodland (ignore a waymark sign to the right) to a stile. Turn left over the stile and up the damp field, past the **standing stone** to a track. Turn right, follow the track over a cattle grid and then turn left up another concession path to the Hanging Stone. Steps to the left lead up to the top and the views. Turn right and follow the path across rough pastures to a gate and wall steps to a path. Turn left down the path to a junction after about 50 metres at a gate/stile. Keep ahead, over the stile, and follow the path, wet in places, for about a kilometre, until a **rocky knoll** appears on the left. Here, take the right fork for about 300 metres to **Lud's Church**.

After your visit, retrace your steps to the knoll and turn right down the path you were originally on. The path descends woods and veers to the right, above the beech tree at the start of the walk, to the ford over **Black Brook**, signposted to **Gradbach**. Over the water, an enchanting, antiquated lane rises to a farm on the right, where a stile gives access to the farmyard. Walk up the yard, keeping immediately left of the farm house to a gate. Follow the track ahead for about 200 metres. Here, the wall on the left turns 90° left, and a concession way also hugs the wall across a rough field to a gate. Although now on access land, helpful concession waymarked posts and a faint trail lead up through the heather and tussocks to the top of the rocky edge. Turn right at the top to the pinnacle and viewpoints on **Gradbach Hill**. Return to the stile at the farm entrance and turn right, keeping ahead on the lane and avoiding the buildings down to the left. This is the Buxton District Scout Camp and you pass their engraved boulder on the left as you descend to join the lane to the

The mossy rocks of Lud's Church (Feb 19) car park, which is about 300 metres ahead.

Fording Black Brook (Feb 19). If you wish to avoid the ford, descend to the footbridge at the start of the walk, cross, rise to the stile and walk uphill from it to the lane.

On the concession path above the Hanging Stone (Jan 25)
Inset. *Looking to Alderley Edge from atop the Hanging Stone (Jan 25)*

Ramshaw Rocks, Baldstones, The Roaches and Hen Cloud

Approaching Red Indian Rock at Ramshaw Rocks (Sept 2)

This circuit of the spectacular rock scenery of the Staffordshire Moorlands starts with an ascent of the jagged crest of Ramshaw rocks; crosses Black Brook Nature Reserve between Baldstones and Gib Torr; rises to The Roaches for an airy traverse of this extraordinary two-tiered gritstone edge; passes the lifeless puddle that is Doxey Pool and ascends lone Hen Cloud before ending with a sedate stroll past the ruins of Dains Mill.

Length 13 kms / 8.13 miles **Map** O/S Explorer OL 24, *White Peak Area*, West Sheet
Start/Finish Lay-by on minor road off the A53 Buxton-Leek road at SK 017 619. This small CP lies at the southern end of Ramshaw Rocks and is not marked on the map.
Terrain Quite a strenuous outing, but route-finding is largely easy along stony tracks and paths, some of which are uphill. Care is needed for the descent of The Roaches, and the paths between Dains Mill and Naychurch are not waymarked on this short section.
Refreshments Pub in Upper Hulme, tea room at Paddock Farm en route to Upper Hulme
When To Go/What's There A bleak walk in winter, but a delight when the heather is in flower. Black Brook NR once had scarce wetland flowers, but a pine wood was planted, the reserve dried, and most of the interest was lost. However, tree felling has started, and it is hoped that the wetlands will be restored. Snipe can still be seen here, and other wildlife includes curlew, skylark, ring ouzel, kestrel and, along Black Brook, the occasional dipper. Stoats are observed along the dry stone walls near Baldstones. However, the most curious resident must be the wallaby. Since escaping from nearby Swythamley Hall they have survived in small numbers for over 60 years. We snapped one in 1987, saw two in 1996, and they were reliably reported in 2002. So they are not extinct yet! **Nearby** *The Winking Man*, a rock that "winks" as you drive north up the A53 past Ramshaw Rocks is losing its flirtatious charm to roadside trees. Management please!

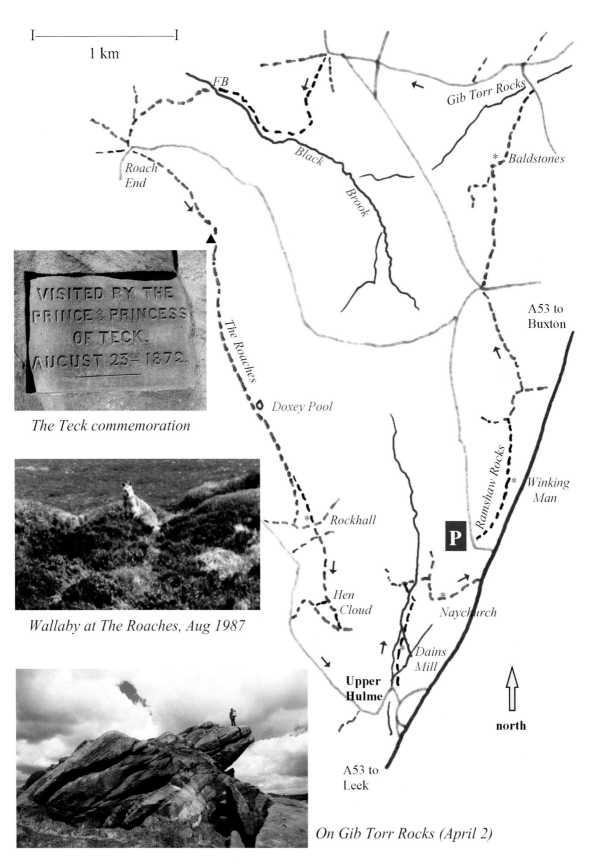

The Teck commemoration

Wallaby at The Roaches, Aug 1987

On Gib Torr Rocks (April 2)

Route From the lay-by, take either of the two paths which lead up to the jagged crest of **Ramshaw Rocks**. Follow the path over the crest and again as it turns left and right to a T-junction. Turn right up the track and leave it at the first junction on a path which leads left across moorland to a minor road. Cross, and take the (not obvious) path which runs to the right of the house and up to and past some rocks to enter Black Brook Nature Reserve at a stile (info board). More rough ground leads to a scenic descent and the prominent rocks of **Baldstones**. Here, the path turns sharp right at a finger post (photo) and leads to a minor road. Go left on the road and left again at a junction, to reach the entrance to **Gib Torr Rocks** on the left. After a visit, return to the road, go straight on at X-roads and again at a junction. After 200 metres, the road turns 90° right. A track goes straight ahead, but don't take it, instead take the track left which leads downhill to cross **Black Brook** via a **footbridge** and eventually uphill to a minor road at **Roach End**. Cross it, and take the path which rises steadily to the trig point. Ahead now gives pleasant walking with expansive views. The path eventually divides, and both descents require a little scrambling (bear right for optional visit to **Rockhall**) before joining the path for an ascent of **Hen Cloud**. From the summit, return to the gap between the crags and descend steeply left to a track. Go right and left at a road to **Upper Hulme**. Here, cross the stream and turn left, passing farms and the ruins of **Dains Mill**, and then turn right at each of two path junctions to reach the track through **Naychurch Farm**. This leads to the **A53**. Turn left and follow the roadside verge uphill to meet the minor road on the left and the lay-by.

Above the steps to Rockhall is a rock seat and inscription commemorating the visit of the Prince and Princess of Teck in 1872. The "Hall", once the home of the piratical-looking Dougie Moller, now houses climbers. Tittesworth Reservoir and Hen Cloud are in view.

Taking the path from Baldstones to Gib Torr Rocks (April 2)

Hen Cloud from the way to Upper Hulme (Aug 22)

31 Cader Low, Pilsbury Castle and The Upper Dove Valley

Looking back to Cader Low during the heat-wave of July 2006

An outing to the upper reaches of The Dove Valley; on two levels, and on both limestone and gritstone - giving rise to wide-ranging scenery. It starts above the village of Hartington and rises across lofty pastures before descending to the banks and natural defences of Pilsbury Castle. The River Dove is crossed to gain height for another panorama, before the route falls to re-cross the river and return sedately back via a lane.

Length 13 kms / 8.13 miles **Map** O/S Explorer OL 24, *White Peak Area*, West Sheet
Start/Finish Hartington, where there is parking in the centre of the village; on the side roads and an "official" car park off the B5054 at SK 127 602. A popular village, go early.
Terrain Up and down farmland paths and tracks and roadwork, largely on a gated lane. After heavy rain or cattle trampling, some paths will be muddy. Could be horses, too.
Refreshments None on route, Hartington village has all outlets.
When To Go/What's There An all-season walk. Pilsbury Castle has information boards. It could date from Norman times and resembled a hill fort. There is a website : *www. pilsburycastle.org.uk* There are small outcrops of limestone pavement, rare in The Peak, on route to Cader Low. The summit tumulus provides a fine panorama. Mountain pansies speckle ancient mine workings. The River Dove is crossed twice: by stepping stones and a footbridge. Lud Well gushes from the limestone and supports bitter-cress and monkey-flower. If it's winter, take a torch and a peep inside the adit to see what's over-wintering. In passing, birds include heron, woodpecker, wheatear, skylark and redstart. The goosanders have been shot. Limestone flowers include thyme, betony, stonecrop, ox-eye daisy, orchids, hawkweeds, geraniums, spleenwort, knapweed and St John's-wort and are visited by common blue, small copper, small heath and skipper butterflies. **Nearby** Hartington itself has much to offer: a cheese factory with retail shop; Victorian pillar-box at the Post Office; pottery workshop and a beautiful Elizabethan hall, now a youth hostel.

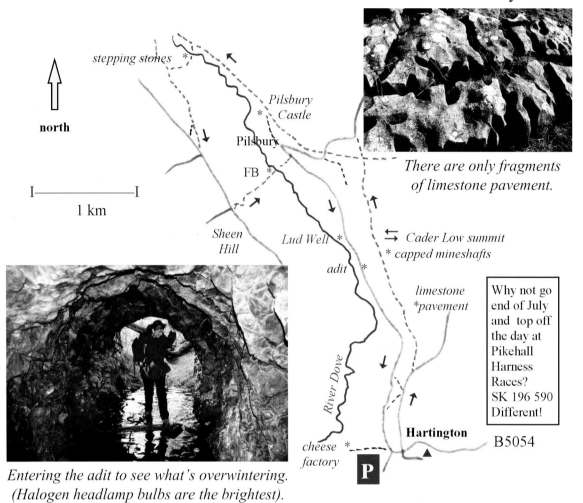

north

I———————I
1 km

stepping stones *

Pilsbury
Castle
*

Pilsbury

FB *

Sheen
Hill

Lud Well *

adit

*

River Dove

cheese *
factory

P

There are only fragments
of limestone pavement.

⇄ Cader Low summit
* capped mineshafts

limestone
*pavement

↓ ↑

Hartington
▲

Why not go
end of July
and top off
the day at
Pikehall
Harness
Races?
SK 196 590
Different!

B5054

Entering the adit to see what's overwintering.
(Halogen headlamp bulbs are the brightest).

Cattle drinking from the R. Dove at the stepping stones (Aug 23). Whilst doing so, many
cows also deposit their waste into the water, thus fuelling eutrophication downstream at
sluggish bays, in which aquatic insect larvae, (trout and dipper food), cannot flourish.

Route Walk up Hind Lane, immediately left of the church. After about ¾ km at a right bend, go over the wall-stile on the left and through three fields with more stiles. Then go through the gate on the left to a track. Follow the track down until it turns sharp left, at which point leave it and enter fields, soon with **limestone pavement**, a little above the path, and posts ahead to show the correct route to a field with capped **mineshafts** and spoil-heaps. Through this field, the way is now clear for an ascent of **Cader Low**, so turn 90° right and walk uphill to the summit. Retrace your steps and continue ahead, over stiles and through fields (noting the waymark angles) for about 1 km, to where the path falls steeply to X-paths. Turn left and pass a standing-stone (there is another beside the road above) to meet a minor road. Cross. Onwards, the way leads across fields and scenically descends to **Pilsbury Castle**, where a gate provides access to the site (information boards). A conspicuous path leads on from the castle through two long fields to two parallel walls with gates and barriers for sheep. Through them, angle left, down to the **River Dove**. Cross the **stepping stones** and stile and walk up to a kissing-gate. A path leads left of a dwelling to its drive. Here, go over the stile on the right, turn left and ascend to two barns, where you turn left to meet the drive again. Follow it up to a sharp bend to the right, where a stile on the left leads to a path over rough land, ending to the right of another dwelling. Walk up this drive to a gate. Go through and, near the top of the drive, leave it at a stile on the left and follow this path through fields to a stile (visible post) at a road. Turn left and walk the road until opposite the second road on the right (signed to *Brund*), then turn left down a rough track to The Dove again. Cross the footbridge and rise to the hamlet of **Pilsbury**. Turn right onto the lane and follow it through a number of gates as it meanders to **Lud Well** spring which feeds The Dove on the right. The **adit** appears on the left soon after Ludwell Farm. Another 2 km stroll leads back to the village of **Hartington**.

On the descent to Pilsbury Castle with the upper Dove Valley beyond (July 24)

Crossing the River Dove (June 12)

Elizabethan Hartington Hall is now a prestige Youth Hostel (May 4)

32 Gypsy Bank, Wolfscote Dale, Biggin Dale and Beresford Dale

Looking down on Gypsy Bank and The Dove Valley from the optional viewpoint (May 23)

A long, but not too strenuous figure-of-eight walk up and down the dales of The Dove Valley. There are a number of exceptional viewpoints, beginning at Gypsy Bank, which is descended to the River Dove. Optional viewpoints and pinnacles are followed by Biggin Dale, Highfield Lane and a 360° panorama. Beresford Dale and all of Wolfscote Dale lead to a viewpoint at Shining Tor, before falling to Viator's Bridge at popular Milldale.

Length 16 kms / 10 miles **Map** O/S Explorer OL 24, *White Peak Area*, West Sheet
Start/Finish Alstonefield Car Park with PCs at SK 130 556. Other car parks in village.
Terrain A mixture of easy paths and tracks, together with fields and, if you opt for the above viewpoint, a steep ascent, mainly off-path. Some paths are steep and some stony.
Refreshments Shop (and PCs) at Milldale; pub at Alstonefield.
When To Go/What's There In May, upper Biggin Dale is alive with early-purple orchids and cowslips. Lower down the dale, the warblers sing above a few of the scarcer plants such as twayblade, broad-leaved and dark-red helleborine and Nottingham catchfly. You may glimpse a green woodpecker. The scree supports little robin and biting stonecrop. Other plants include thyme, saw-wort, trefoils, scabious, knapweed, violet, meadow saxifrage and gorse. Ten species of butterfly include dingy skipper, brimstone, comma and northern brown argus near rock-rose. There has been a resident heron in Wolfscote Dale for many years. Dippers here, too. Other birds en route include goldfinch, skylark, curlew, wheatear, pied and yellow wagtail and redstart. If you visit the short caves at the start of Wolfscote Dale (map), the "hidden", upper cave has concretions. In Beresford Dale there is a fallen tree trunk that has sprouted money, but Pike Pool disappoints. Woods at the start of the walk have pink parslane in May/June. **Nearby** The summits of Gratton Hill and Narrowdale Hill are now attainable on access land.

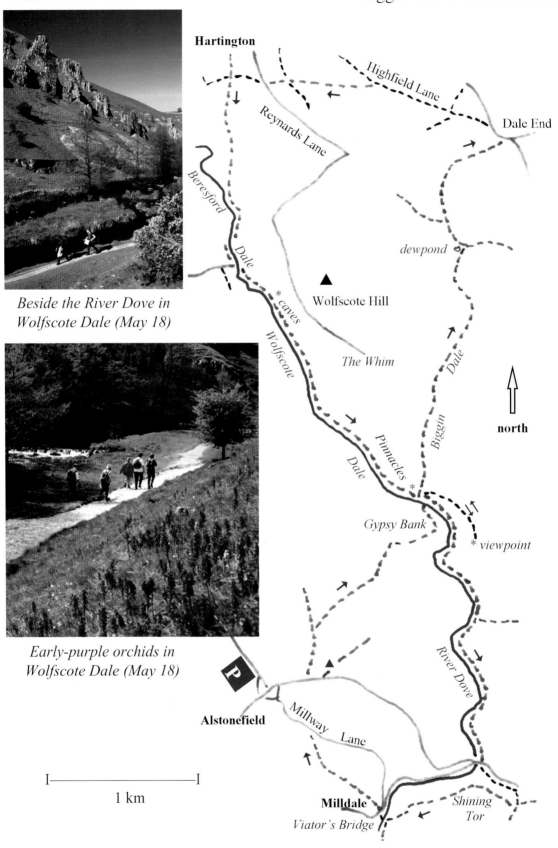

*Beside the River Dove in
Wolfscote Dale (May 18)*

*Early-purple orchids in
Wolfscote Dale (May 18)*

1 km

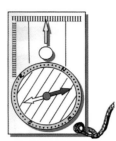

Route Cross the road and turn right. Stay on this pavement as it passes an old chapel and leaves the village. After 200 metres, turn left onto a track. After about 300 metres turn right at the fork, where there is a signpost to **Gypsy Bank**. The path enters a farm and, soon after, slants 45° left across a field, to a stile. The way now leads to the top of Gypsy Bank where there are fine views. A steep descent leads to a footbridge over the **River Dove**. Turn left, go through a gate to a stone squeezer stile. (If you wish to climb to the **viewpoint** pictured on p.163, go up the faint path which rises from the dale bottom, a few metres before the squeezer stile, and keep climbing and slanting right until the view is attained. The detour will add about ¾ hour to your day). Go through the stile and turn right. This is the start of **Biggin Dale**. (A way to the **pinnacles** on the left appears after a few metres). Follow the stony path up the dale through gates to reach a path junction at a **dew pond** on the left. Turn left here through a gate, and ahead another junction is met after a couple of hundred metres or so. Keep straight on and go over a stile to eventually emerge on a minor road at **Dale End**. Go left and immediately left again up a track, **Highfield Lane**. About ½ km after X-tracks, leave the track on the left and go through fields/stiles to a track. Go right and immediately

Watching a twister develop over Wolfscote Dale (July 29)

left down track to a lane. Go right then left between farm buildings down another track to where footpaths cross it after about 200 metres. Turn left through the stile and follow the path as it crosses fields to **Beresford Dale**. Two footbridges span The Dove. After the second, walk across a wet field to another stile at the start of **Wolfscote Dale (caves** up to the left). The prominent path is now followed all the way downstream, passing the entrance to Biggin Dale again, and eventually reaching a road. Cross and turn left up the concessionary path until it meets the public footpath on the left. Here, turn 90° right and uphill to X-paths. Turn right and follow the path to **Shining Tor**, which is opposite the end of Wolfscote Dale. (Walk out right for view). The path joins another and descends into **Milldale**. Cross **Viator's Bridge** and head across the road to the shop. A few metres past, a stile and path on the left lead uphill to fields. The incline gradually eases, and you emerge onto **Millway Lane**. Turn left, passing the church and then the pub on the left on the way back to the CP at **Alstonefield**.

Approaching Wolfscote Dale from the bottom of Biggin Dale (May 18)

Looking down on walkers in Wolfscote Dale from the pinnacles at the bottom of Biggin Dale (June 10). **Inset.** *Common twayblade in Biggin Dale (June 10)*

33 | Elderbush Cave, Thor's Cave, Nan Tor Cave and Wetton Hill

Atop Thor's Cave Crag (Sept 24). **Inset.** *Wood anemones in the woods below (April 19)*

This outing to the caves and hills of The Manifold Valley, departs Wetton and explores Seven Ways Cave and Elderbush Cave before reaching the huge opening of Thor's Cave. A descent into the valley, and a short detour to Ladyside for the views, is followed by a stroll to Nan Tor Cave at Wetton Mill; a secluded dale and an ascent of Wetton Hill.

Length 8 Kms / 5 miles **Map** O/S Explorer OL 24, *White Peak Area*, West Sheet
Start/Finish Wetton CP and PCs at SK 108 551. There is an adjacent campsite.
Terrain Some steep, stony and potentially slippery places have to be taken with care, but the majority of the route is easy. There is a vertical drop from atop Thor's Cave Crag.
Refreshments Shop/café at Wetton Mill. Pub at Wetton (both not always open).
When To Go/What's There The caves and dramatic scenery are of interest all year round, but a visit in snow/ice is not advisable. Some "windows" of Seven Ways Cave can be seen from atop Thor's Cave Crag, but enter from behind. Elderbush Cave, which lies lower than Seven Ways in a depression near a hawthorn tree, has profuse spleenwort, crinoid fossils, concretions and, unusually, sample bore holes into rock and even into the only surviving stalagmite. Pleistocene to Romano-British finds are on display in Buxton Museum. The rocks at the entrance to Thor's Cave and its "window" have become polished due to countless boots, and these few metres can be tricky, especially when wet. In early spring, there are primroses, bluebells and wood anemones in the woods beneath Thor's Cave, and mountain pansies speckle the flanks of Wetton Hill. In summer, orpine, bellflowers, scabious, St.John's-wort, knapweed, lady's bedstraw, harebells, betony and umbellifers flower on Thor's Cave Crag; and this rich assemblage attracts at least seven species of butterfly. The route beside The Manifold supports water avons, red campion, butterbur, marsh marigolds and forget-me-nots. **Nearby** Butterton is a charming village with a ford flowing down the street; farm produce to buy and *The Black Swan* to relax in.

Sugarloaf

Nan Tor Cave
at Wetton Mill

R. Manifold

Wetton
Hill *

Hoo

Brook

Wetton

Ladyside
Wood

viewpoint *

P

Thor's Cave

north

I————————I

1 km

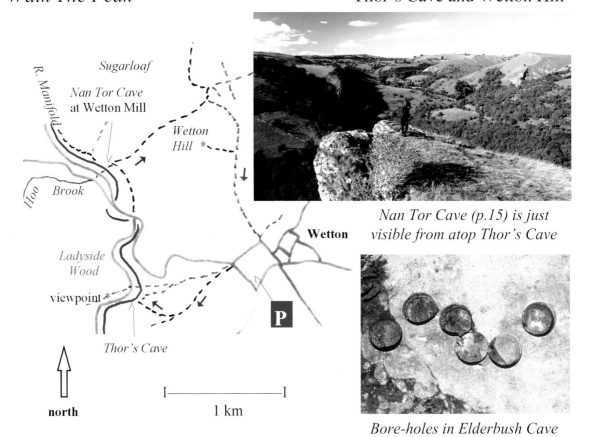

*Nan Tor Cave (p.15) is just
visible from atop Thor's Cave*

Bore-holes in Elderbush Cave

Sugarloaf (left) and Wetton Hill from the Ladyside viewpoint (Nov 22)

Route Turn right out of the car park and then right down the side road to a T-junction. Turn left and very soon left again down a track. There is currently a concession path sign to **Thor's Cave** here. On the skyline, Grindon church steeple is now in view, with Thor's Cave Crag beneath. After about ½ km, and after a gate/stile, climb the wall stile on the right. Turn left down the field and up another to a gate/fence. If you want to see the view from atop the crag as per p.167 then walk left up the path to the top of the crag. Seven Ways Cave and Elderbush Cave are to be found in depressions away from the top of the crag. To only visit Thor's Cave (equally good view) walk down from the gate and up the few steps to the entrance. The "West Window" can be seen on the right wall. Steps and a path lead down from Thor's Cave through woodland to meet another path. Turn left and cross the **River Manifold** by the footbridge. Ahead, a stile gives access to the viewpoint on the way to **Ladyside Wood**. If you decline, turn right on the single track road which crosses The Manifold again. Take the right fork to **Wetton Mill**, which is attained by turning right over the bridge. A footpath leads between buildings right of the café to **Nan Tor Cave** on the left (p.15) and, to the right, over fields and stiles and down to the path which runs up the dale between **Sugarloaf** and **Wetton Hill**. Turn left up the dale, which has expanding views behind. At the top of the dale, go through the gate/stile and, after about 20 metres, turn right through the wall stile. The path crosses a stream and leads uphill to run to the left of a wall. Near to the top of the incline, the path reaches a wooden stile. To the right, steps in the wall offer the easiest ascent of Wetton Hill. Over the stile, the way leads on over fields and through narrow stiles to reach a farm track, which is followed straight on and down to a road. Walk ahead, passing the phone booth on the right and then *Ye Olde Royal Oak*, also on the right, before turning right once more to the car park at **Wetton**.

Walkers dwarfed by the huge entrance to Thor's Cave (June 10). It was originally known as Thyrsis's Cavern. Finds from caves on this walk are in Buxton Museum.

*Wetton Hill and the Manifold Valley
from Seven Ways Cave (Sept 24)*

Parapenting tuition on the flanks of Wetton Hill (July 16)

34 Thorpe Cloud, Dovedale High Level Route and Bunster Hill

Thorpe Cloud from Thorpe Pastures, showing the easy way up to the summit (Feb 5)

This short but strenuous circuit of Dovedale National Nature Reserve takes you to most of the renowned sights but is mainly off the main tourist path that runs the whole length of the dale. In addition, we have three fine aerial views. The route takes the easy way up Thorpe Cloud, descends to the Stepping Stones, immediately rises to high above the dale, then undulates before gradually descending to the Dove Holes and Ilam Rock. A steep ascent of Dovedale Wood is followed by a thrilling traverse and descent of Bunster Hill.

Length 9 kms / 5.6 miles **Map** O/S Explorer OL 24, *White Peak Area*, West Sheet
Start/Finish The National Trust car park in Dovedale at SK 146 509 (fee)
Terrain An undulating walk, mainly on well-defined paths, some of which are stony and may have nettles in summer. The uphill path through Dovedale Wood to Air Cottage can be slippery when wet, and the airy descent from Bunster Hill has to be taken with care.
Refreshments Weekend and summer café at the car park. Short drive to Ilam Hall (teas).
When To Go/What's There A walk for all seasons. The limestone gorge is most visible when the leaves are off the trees, but there is obviously more wildlife interest in spring and summer. Goosanders and grey wagtails are a regular sight on The Dove, along with dippers, which nest safely in the cave roofs. The damp caves support liverworts and spleenwort. From the high-level route the summer birdsong rises from the woods, and birds such as green woodpecker, heron, buzzard and kestrel may float across the dale. We have frequently counted twelve species of butterfly, but it is the flora which is most diverse. There are scarce shrubs such as spindle, mountain current and mezereon; and more readily identifiable plants such as harebells, hawkweeds, thyme, orpine, mullein, rock-rose, cornsalad, herb-Paris, violet and marjoram. Dovedale is exceptionally busy on summer weekends and bank holidays, but annual figures quoted (2 million!), are alarmist.
Nearby Tissington has a fine hall, and its well-dressings are legendary. Bradbourne has a popular ford (SK 199 521) and a repaired Saxon cross in the churchyard (SK 207 527).

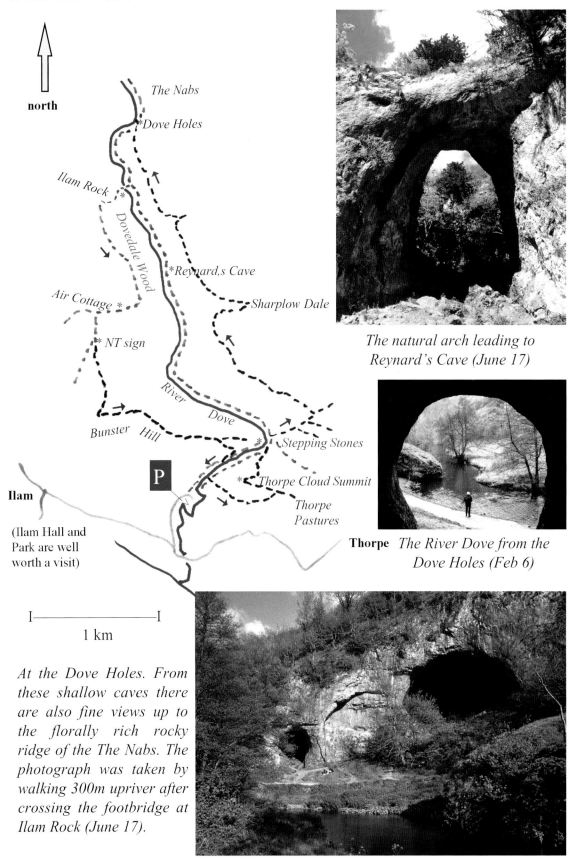

north

The Nabs

*Dove Holes

Ilam Rock *

Dovedale Wood

*Reynard,s Cave

Air Cottage *

Sharplow Dale

* NT sign

River Dove

Bunster Hill

P

Stepping Stones

Ilam

* Thorpe Cloud Summit

(Ilam Hall and
Park are well
worth a visit)

Thorpe
Pastures

I———————————I
1 km

The natural arch leading to
Reynard's Cave (June 17)

Thorpe *The River Dove from the
Dove Holes (Feb 6)*

*At the Dove Holes. From
these shallow caves there
are also fine views up to
the florally rich rocky
ridge of the The Nabs. The
photograph was taken by
walking 300m upriver after
crossing the footbridge at
Ilam Rock (June 17).*

Route Turn right out of the car park and soon right again over the footbridge across the **River Dove**. Continue ahead between fencing. The path gradually rises and eventually swings left to join the path up the SE face of **Thorpe Cloud** from **Thorpe Pastures**. Ascend to the rocky summit and walk ahead along the ridge. At the end of the ridge, turn right down a path which descends steeply. There is a rocky section at the bottom. The path brings you out just right of the popular **Stepping Stones**. Ahead is a gate and two stone stiles. Go through and turn immediately right up a faint path that runs uphill to the left of a wall. Continue up past two ladder stiles to a fence. Here, turn left and ascend to the summit of the hill (viewpoint, below). From here, the path runs left of a wall, high above the dale. It leads to a gate, contours around **Sharplow Dale**, falls to a stile in another dale and then undulates on its descent through woodland to the **Dove Holes**. After a visit to the caves, turn left on the path beside The Dove to a footbridge just before **Ilam Rock**. If you wish an easier finish to the walk, continue on the path, passing Lion Rock, **Reynard's Cave** and Tissington Spires en route to the Stepping Stones and, onwards, the car park. Otherwise, cross the footbridge, turn right and, after about 200 metres, turn left up a path (signposted **Ilam**). The path winds up through **Dovedale Wood** and turns left to run along the top of the wood. As you exit the wood, ahead and down to the left is a footpath post. Head to this and follow waymarks and finger-posts to emerge through two gates on the drive to **Air Cottage**. Turn left, then left again beside an avenue of sycamore trees. Gates and fields lead to the NT sign for **Bunster Hill**. Walk ahead, uphill and soon bear right to the three summit hillocks. From the highest, the undulating descent ridge can be seen at a lower level, ahead and to the left. Keep to the right of the wall that heads to the start of the ridge, crossing two wooden stiles to gain the ridge. Follow the path down the undulations. Near the end of the ridge, look for an indistinct path that leads down left, being careful not to go over the last hummock. The path becomes more prominent as it leads left, across and down a grassy bank. Where it forks, just past the pointed summit of Thorpe Cloud, which is on your right, bear right, steeply down. The path veers to the right of a rocky outcrop and descends to the path in the dale bottom. Turn right to the car park.

Bunster Hill from nearby Ilam (Sept 2)

Climbers tackling the pinnacle of Ilam Rock (June 17)
Inset. *The busy Stepping Stones taken from near the bottom of Bunster Hill (July 20)*

35 Beeston Tor, Mere Hill, Throwley Old Hall and Castern Wood NR

Old Park Hill (left) and Soles Hill from Larkstone Lane (July 3)
Inset. *Mushroom growing from an ancient hawthorn tree at Throwley (Sept 4)*

This aerial circuit of the River Manifold passes Beeston Tor crag before rising to Mere Hill and an expansive panorama. A visit to the romantic ruins of Throwley Old Hall is followed by a scenic descent. Above the valley lies Castern Hall, and beyond, the path above Castern Wood Nature Reserve surely is one of the promenades of the White Peak.

Length 13 kms / 8.13 miles **Map** O/S Explorer OL 24, *White Peak Area*, West Sheet
Start/Finish Weag's Bridge car park, 1½ kms SW of Wetton at SK 099 542
Terrain Farm paths, tracks and roads. Some indistinct or muddy paths over farmland.
Refreshments Weekend/summer van at the car park.
When To Go/What's There Beeston Tor is alive with crow species and, at the weekend, rock climbers. There are two information boards and a seat at 16th century Throwley Old Hall. Ancient mine workings, ridge and furrow fields and lynchets speckle the landscape. Some of the views are breathtaking. In early spring, plants include butterbur, dog's mercury, wood anemone, primrose, violet, gorse, blackthorn and marsh marigold. Later, harebell, yarrow, hawkweeds, geraniums and knapweed bloom. There are many ancient ash and hawthorn trees. When the warblers arrive, the birdsong in the valley is symphonic. Buzzards float above and, before you see them, you may hear the cackle of the green woodpecker and the drumming of the great-spotted. Skylark, wheatear, blackcap and yellowhammer are more conspicuous. Butterflies abound, and bats flit by on summer evenings. The Hamps and Manifold rivers are frequently dry due to the very porous nature of the local limestone and the many fissures it holds. The latter bubbles up in Ilam Park. **Nearby** There is a unique road tunnel near Swainsley. Apes Tor and other limestone outcrops on the *Manifold Way* exhibit massive rock folding.

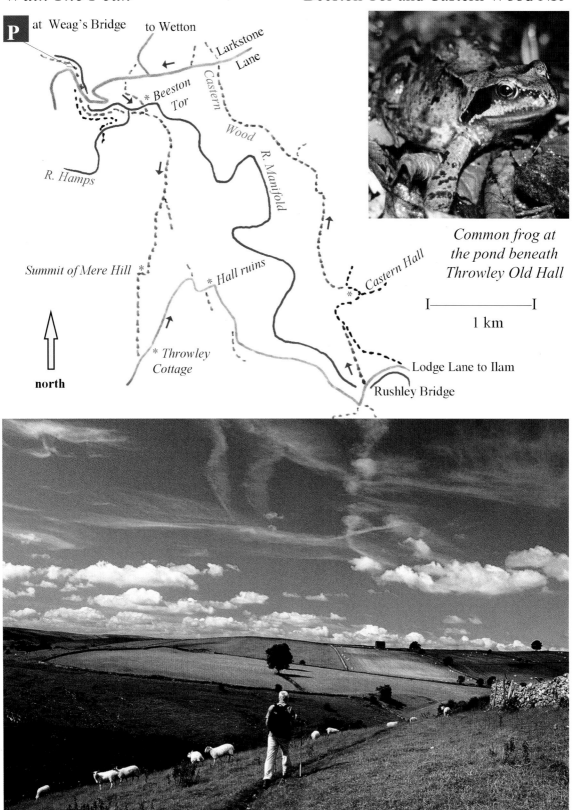

P at Weag's Bridge

to Wetton

Larkstone Lane

Castern Wood

* Beeston Tor

R. Manifold

R. Hamps

Summit of Mere Hill *

* Hall ruins

* Castern Hall

* Throwley Cottage

north

Rushley Bridge

Lodge Lane to Ilam

1 km

Common frog at the pond beneath Throwley Old Hall

Approaching Larkstone Lane from the path above Castern Wood Nature Reserve (Aug 3)

Route Turn left out of car park and take the left of two lanes that run to the right of the **River Manifold**. This leads through an odd caravan park and over the **River Hamps** at its confluence with The Manifold. About 50m on, a gate leads to the river where you must check if it is fordable for the end of the walk. About 50m past the gate, turn right off the lane and up a track, which soon becomes grassy. At the second gate/stile, ignore the waymark sign pointing left and continue ahead, uphill, passing field systems on the left. At a wall, ignore the footpath sign and continue up beside the wall to a gate/wall stile and then to another, 50m ahead. Through this set, angle about 45° right until the wall swings right, then go leftish uphill to the summit of **Mere Hill**. From here, turn right and follow the wall down to a wide gap in the wall. Turn left, and walk ahead across the fields, aiming for the right end of a plantation, before which, a minor road is reached. Turn left, pass **Throwley Cottage** on the right, and follow the road down to the **ruins** of Throwley Old Hall and onwards to the

Throwley Old Hall from the lane to Rushley

River Manifold again at **Rushley Bridge**. Turn left over the bridge and cross three fields with stiles to a road. Turn left up the road to **Castern Hall**, which occasionally opens to the public. Round the hall and leave the road at a right hand bend, taking the track on the left to a gate/stile. Fields lead to two more gates/stiles. After the second, follow the right track uphill to another gate/stile with a small standing stone. Cross the field ahead to the left hand corner, go through a gate and angle left to another gate and small stile. Turn right and walk above **Castern Wood** Nature Reserve, crossing fields and stiles to meet a road, **Larkstone Lane**. Go left, down the road (narrow verges) until, about 150m past the turning to Wetton on the right, there is a stile on the left. If the River Manifold was impassable following your recce at the start of the walk, keep on the road, which spirals down to **Weag's Bridge**. If the river was empty or fordable, go over the stile and follow the path down to the foot of Beeston Tor. Cross the riverbed, go through the gate and turn right to the car park at Weag's Bridge.

Beeston Tor, with a full River Manifold (May 26)

At the ruins of Throwley Old Hall (Feb 5). There are interesting stone window seats and fireplaces, together with floor emplacements to see, but also some teetering stones above!

Walks On White Peak Map ——————— East Sheet
(Explorer Outdoor Leisure Series No 24)

A frosty morning beside the River Wye at Rowsley (Walk 45, Dec 22)

36 Bretton Clough, Abney Clough and Eyam Moor

On the path over Eyam Moor (Aug 22)

It is said that you can see five counties from the Barrel Inn at Bretton. Whether this is before or after your visit to the hostelry is open to debate! However, this view is one of a number of fine panoramas seen on our walk through a rugged landscape. We also visit a Neolithic cup-marked stone and an ancient, initialled boulder prepared for splitting.

Length 13 kms / 8.13 miles **Map** O/S Explorer OL 24, *White Peak Area*, East Sheet
Start/Finish Roadside parking near the *Barrel Inn* at Bretton (SK 200 779).
Terrain Easy to follow paths and tracks over moors and pastures. Some may be muddy.
Refreshments The *Barrel Inn* or your packed lunch.
When to Go/What's There In Abney Clough, speckled wood, small copper, common blue, red admiral, and small heath butterflies fly, and great-spotted woodpeckers feed at the numerous ant hills. Goldcrests visit the larches, and long-tailed tits and goldfinches flit by. In autumn, squirrels feed on the hazel nuts. Flowers include marsh pennywort, creeping Jenny, trailing St-John's-wort, sheep's-bit, foxgloves and saw-wort. You may smell fox, glimpse weasel and watch rabbit. Vocal birds include skylark, lapwing, curlew and summer warblers. Abney itself has a Victorian postbox. The ling heather on Eyam Moor harbours bell heather, cross-leaved heath, cotton-grass, bilberry and compact rush and also a number of burial cairns, one of which contains the cup-marked stone. There is a fine stand of ragged-robin beside the FB to Abney. The *Split Stone* is engraved with the stonemason's initials and his brother started and claimed the boulder below. There are medieval clearance cairns beside Newfoundland Nursery. Rambling builders have been busy at Stoke Ford where stone seats now reside. **Nearby** in Eyam churchyard is a fine 8th century Saxon cross. This over-popular village also has stocks and a fine hall, but is morbidly most famous for the heroics of its 17th century plague victims. *Mompesson's Well*, the *Riley Graves* and the annual Plague Service in The Delf should set the scene.

Photographed during a squall, a rare double rainbow over Bretton Clough, taken from the lane to Nether Bretton and ...

... on the path into the clough five minutes later (both Oct 17)

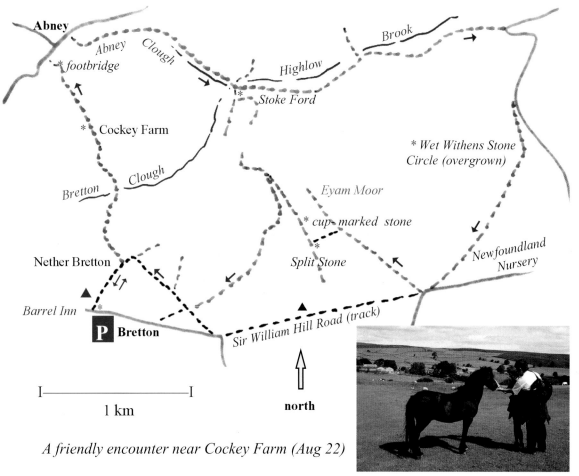

A friendly encounter near Cockey Farm (Aug 22)

Ascending the Split Stone for a lunchtime perch (Sept 2)

Route Walk past the **Barrel Inn** on the right and, immediately after, turn right down a lane. Pass the **Youth Hostel** on the left and about 250m on, turn left, off the lane and on to a footpath which runs intrusively right of a dwelling. A stile brings open fields and stiles on the left; a path through gorse and steps down to **Bretton Clough**. At a post, the way right is now open for an exploration of the interesting ruins and hummocks in the clough, but the route leads ahead on a path which veers to the right then left, before dropping down to streams, which are crossed via a pair of footbridges. The path now leads up through bracken to open fields and **Cockey Farm**, where waymarks lead to more fields and ultimately a track, which is soon exited right where the somewhat inconspicuous path drops down to a footbridge and up to the road at **Abney**. Turn right, and about 200m later, right again down a footpath which leads, eventually, into **Abney Clough** (beware of a tempting wrong path off right) and ultimately, to **Stoke Ford**. Here, cross **Highlow Brook** by the footbridge (ignore the path right to Eyam) and proceed ahead up through ancient oaks then over open land to another ford. Ahead is ever-maturing woodland but the path eventually emerges into pleasant fields, at the end of which a road is met. Go right, uphill

The cup-marked stone on Eyam Moor (Sept 2)

for about ½ km to a footpath on the right which leads pleasantly up to the junction of a minor road and **Sir William Hill Road**. Go over the wall stile to the road, turn right and immediately climb another wall stile on the right. The path leads through heather, until three large boulders can be seen above on the left. When level with them, a path leads up to the **Split Stone**. 50m on, turn right down a path. After about 200m, the **Cup Stone** itself lies in a conspicuous small crater about 10m off to the right. The path now leads down to a gate and stile. Ignore them and turn 90° left on the path which runs to the left of a wall, skirts a small pine wood and leads to a track. Follow this to X-tracks, turn right, and this track soon merges into the lane which leads to the *Barrel Inn* again which is usually open all day.

37 Padley Gorge, Longshaw, White Edge and Froggatt Edge

The trig pillar on White Edge (Aug 8)

This long, scenic but not too strenuous ramble starts through Padley Gorge, with its ancient woodland and tumbling stream; enters the Longshaw Estate where there is a fine wildlife lake; gently rises for an airy traverse of White Edge; descends to Curbar Edge and returns via the popular Froggatt Edge, visiting Tumbling Hill and Tegness Pinnacle.

Length 15 kms / 9.4 miles **Map** O/S Explorer OL 24, *White Peak Area*, East Sheet
Start/Finish The slip road to Grindleford Station (and café) at SK 250 786
Terrain Easy walking on paths, but short sections may be boggy, slippery or stony.
Refreshments Legendary café at the CP; w/end café at Longshaw; occ van, Curbar Gap.
When To Go/What's There In spring, the dippers, woodpeckers, warblers and pied flycatchers come alive in Padley Gorge, together with the ants, bluebells, squirrels and wood sorrel. At Tumbling Hill and Tegness, the summer visiting ring ouzel can be seen; cuckoos heard and bilberries picked amidst the heath bedstraw and climbing corydalis. Perhaps basking in sunshine near the trig pillar on White Edge could be the occasional adder, lizard or field tiger beetle. Skylarks sing, too, and you may glimpse the renegade herd of red deer that colonised Big Moor from Chatsworth. Seven species of dragonfly rise from Longshaw Lake, including the distinctive 4-spot chaser, and the large red and emerald damselflies. The marshy areas of the estate have lousewort and skullcap; in June the rhododendron bloom and, near to The Lodge, there are commemorative plaques, stones and a 1787 guide stoop. (Toilets, too). In autumn, Padley Gorge is host to mosses, lichens and many species of fungi, including the delicious Cep. However, there are a number of deadly species including The Destroying Angel, Death Cap and Blusher, so keep an eye on the kids. A small stone circle is passed on Froggatt Edge and navelwort just survives below. **Nearby** on route to White Edge, a detour could be made to *Lady's Cross*, but there is little to see except bird droppings on the small 17th century stump.

Looking out over the bell and ling heather from the top of Curbar Edge (Aug 8)

Higger Tor from the lake at Longshaw (July 23). When fully frozen in winter, ice skaters have fun. **Inset.** *Navelwort just clings to existence beneath the Eastern Edges (June 9).*

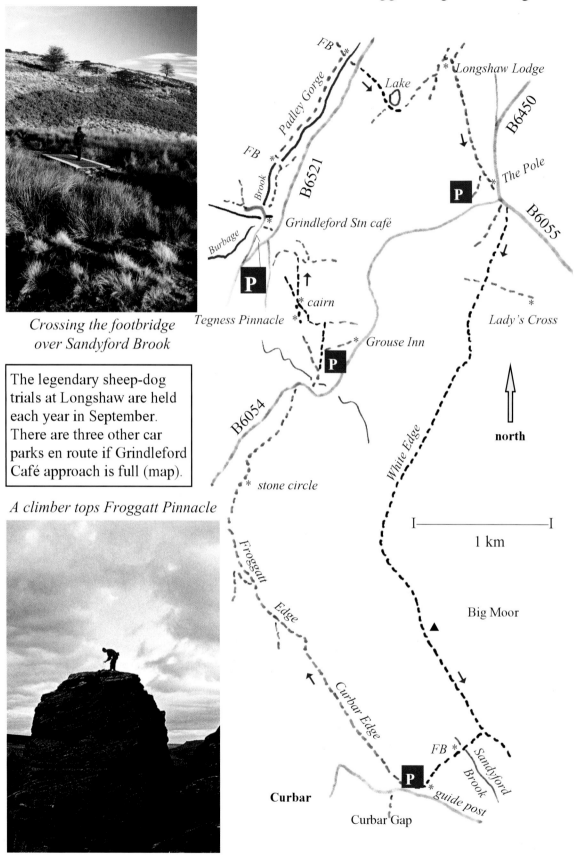

Crossing the footbridge over Sandyford Brook

The legendary sheep-dog trials at Longshaw are held each year in September. There are three other car parks en route if Grindleford Café approach is full (map).

A climber tops Froggatt Pinnacle

Route Pass the café, cross the railway line and turn right through the stile. Soon leave the main path and follow those nearer **Burbage Brook** so as not to miss the footbridge. Cross the **FB** and rise to the main path through **Padley Gorge**. Turn right and follow this path through and out of the woods to another **FB**. Cross it and rise to the **B6521**. Cross the road and enter the Longshaw Estate. Follow the path as it rounds the **lake** and leads beside rhododendrons to a junction. Turn left to **Longshaw Lodge**. Go up the track immediately left of the lodge and turn right on the track behind the lodge. Further on, views right and to the rear open up. Where the grassy path forks, keep left to **The Pole**, which may be still standing. Here, cross the 3-way road junction and go over the stile ahead into access land (ignore the gate down to the right). About 400 metres up the path, at a low, waymarked post, a path leads off left to *Lady's Cross*. Onwards, the path reaches the trig pillar on **White Edge** after about 3 kms. It is a little left of the path. After about another kilometre and, where the path meets a wall on the right, turn right down a path (currently signed to **Curbar Gap**). Cross the **FB** over **Sandyford Brook** and follow the path to the car park, noting the **guide post** to *"Sheffield Roade"* (and a *"V"*). Go up steps in the top left of the CP and follow the path as it bears right to a gate. Once through, leave the main path and walk left to follow the climbers' path along the top of **Curbar Edge**, where there are

Bell heather above Tegness Pinnacle (May 28)

millstones and views. The path ahead leads above **Froggatt Edge**, passes The Pinnacle and a small **stone circle** on the right and reaches the **B6054**. Turn right and soon cross the road opposite a stile. Walk down to and cross a stream. Keep on this path as it passes a CP on the right. Go over a stile and walk ahead, ignore path down left, and follow the path until the wall on the right turns 90° right. Here, turn left and follow this path to the **cairn** on Tumbling Hill. (**Tegness Pinnacle** is reached by turning left here, and following the narrow path along the top of the edge for about 200 metres. Return). Ahead of the cairn is a fine viewpoint. Now descend on the path right to a gate on the right. This gives access to open fields and leads left to gates through two adjacent walls. Walk ahead to a path T-junction. Turn left and follow the path down the woods to a lane. Turn right to reach the **B6521**. Cross, turn right then left down the path to **Grindleford Station café**.

38   Coombs Dale, The Roman Baths and Calver Weir

Bluebell, red campion and gorse beside the path to Coombs Dale (May 22)
Inset. *Peacock butterfly on Froggatt Bridge (July 13)*

This short walk rises above Calver, with views to Bretton, Chatsworth, Minninglow and Higger Tor; enters a short, secluded dale into Coombs Dale; rises to Stoney Middleton then falls to the Roman Baths; rises again for an uninterrupted view of Curbar and Froggatt Edges before falling to the River Derwent for a waterside amble past Calver Weir.

Length 9 kms / 5.6 miles **Map** O/S Explorer OL 24, *White Peak Area*, East Sheet
Start/Finish Cul-de-sac off A623 at Calver, adjacent to infant school at SK 247 743
Terrain Easy paths, tracks and a little roadwork. The path to the weir is often muddy.
Refreshments *Moon Inn* and shop at Stoney Middleton; café, shop and pubs at Calver
When To Go/What's There As you near the B6001 at the start of the walk, three stone troughs are unusually protected by an arched stone roof. There is an information board at the (probably not) Roman Baths. Signs tell us that Calver Weir is becoming unstable. It was created to provide a consistent water supply for Calver Mill (now apartments) which became Colditz Castle for the TV series. Water vole, tufted duck, little grebe, heron, and goosander roam the River Derwent. In winter, bullfinch, goldfinch, jay and fieldfare become conspicuous and goldcrest visit the pines at Froggatt Bridge. Coombs Dale supports orange-tip, northern brown argus, dingy skipper, small copper and common blue butterflies on the herb-rich grasslands, where orchids, cowslip, rock-rose, spring sandwort, bird's-foot trefoil, pepper-saxifrage, thyme, meadow saxifrage, dark-red helleborine, milkwort, mossy saxifrage and violets flower. The swamp near New Bridge supports frogs, greater butterfly-orchid, yellow flag, southern marsh-orchid and yellow loosestrife. A pond dug here will soon mature. **Nearby** there is a fine walk through Bank Wood and Bramley Wood. The latter is ablaze with rhododendron in May (SK 241 739).

Rock-rose and pepper-saxifrage on the florally rich bank-side out of Coombs Dale (May 31). **Inset.** *Oxlip (in The Peak a hybrid of primrose and cowslip) flowers earlier (April 9).*

On the path to New Bridge beside the River Derwent (Jan 6)

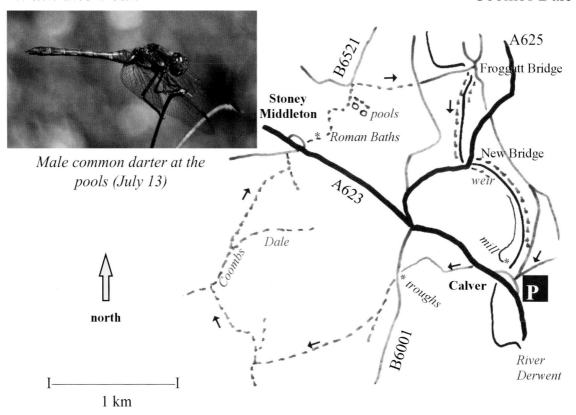

Male common darter at the pools (July 13)

north

I————————I
1 km

New Bridge from Calver Weir (Oct 21). Water voles and herons are often seen here.

Route From the cul-de-sac, pass the *Bridge Inn* on your left; cross the **River Derwent** by the footbridge; pass the craft centre on your right and cross to the other side of the **A623**. Turn right and soon left into the lane to **Calver** village. Walk up the village; pass the village hall on the left and later the covered water **troughs** on your left as you near the **B6001**. Cross the road and climb the stile ahead. The path now slants left, uphill until it runs into a track. Continue up the track until it forks. Take the right fork and the track soon becomes a path.

The way ahead is now over stiles and grazing land to where scrub can be seen in the distance. Head to the left end of the last field, climb the stile and enter the scrub. About 50 metres on, turn right and follow the path downhill. After another stile, turn left into the start of a valley. Near the bottom, a stile on the left also leads to the track that runs up **Coombs Dale**. Turn right down the track. After about 300 metres, turn left and over a stile amidst hawthorns. Soon the path opens out and slants right and then uphill to another stile. This leads to open fields and stiles to farm buildings, which you keep on your right, to meet a minor road. Turn right, downhill to the A623 at **Stoney Middleton**. Cross the main road and go down The Nook (lane); pass the church on the right; the old water pump on the left, to reach the **Roman Baths** (picnic site above). Ahead, the lane becomes a cinder track and climbs steadily. Just before it reaches the **B6521**, a footpath right leads to two pools (dragonflies and water birds), but the way continues up the track to the road, where a stile on the right leads to fields and down to the B6001. Cross and walk down the lane to **Froggatt Bridge**. Don't cross but climb the stile on the right and follow the waterside path. Pass willow swamp on the right; cross a FB and reach **New Bridge**. Turn left, cross The Derwent, and immediately right through a stile. The path passes the **weir** and eventually reaches a road. Turn right and pass the **mill** to soon reach the *Bridge Inn*.

A frosty day at Froggatt Bridge (Jan 6)

Early-purple orchids and Peter's Stone at the head of Cressbrook Dale (June 7)

Cressbrook Dale is the most evocative of all the Derbyshire Dales National Nature Reserves. This excursion leads you through its highlights, including an explosive view of the dale from Wardlow, and to three other florally and scenically rich satellite dales.

Length 12 kms / 7.5 miles **Map** O/S Explorer OL 24, *White Peak Area*, East Sheet
Start/Finish Tideswell Dale Car Park (Picnic tables & WC) at SK 154 742
Terrain The route is easy to follow, but there are short, rocky sections in Cressbrook Dale and Tansley Dale, which have to be negotiated with care in slippery conditions.
Refreshments Pub & café at Wardlow Mires; pub at Wardlow.
When To Go/What's There The woodlands, scrub, herbs and grasses have given Cressbrook Dale a unique floral composition. Although there are rarities such as yellow star-of-Bethlehem, green hellebore and bird's-foot sedge, it is the stands of early-purple orchids, cowslips and wood anemones that most attract the walker in springtime. Stemless thistle, water avens, violets, hairy rock-cress, meadow and mossy saxifrage and bird cherry are readily seen, and spring sandwort and alpine penny-cress can be found at some galena spoil heaps. Bluebells, ramsons and dog's mercury are mainly in the woods. Unusually, in the warm April of 2007, nearly all the flowers were in bloom at the same time. Exmoor ponies were introduced to graze the scrub but began by munching the orchids near Peter's Stone! Birds include kestrel, wheatear, long-tailed tit, skylark and green woodpecker. Water voles and trout are observed in the Wye at Miller's Dale. Peter's Stone has a macabre history, but the outcrops beneath it have some fine examples of fossilised crinoids. There are four wood sculptures by Andrew Frost near the car park.
Nearby Tideswell's well dressings and torchlight procession are worth a visit and there is a fine wayside cross in a farmyard at Wheston, sadly becoming evermore overgrown.

A climber on the imposing overhanging crag at Ravenstor (Aug 2)
Inset. *Bloody cranes-bill beside the road to the crag (Aug 2)*

Bird cherry (June 7)

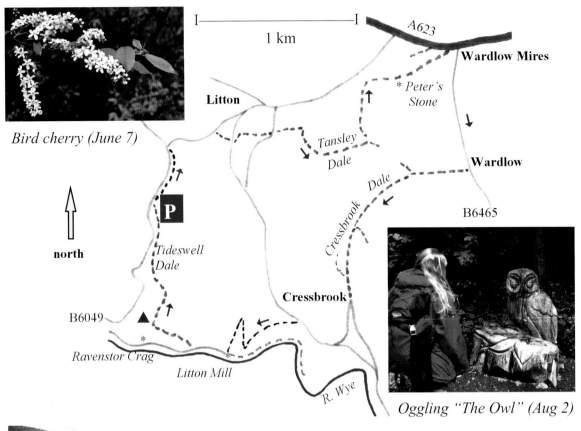

Oggling "The Owl" (Aug 2)

Passing Peter's Stone (June 7). Fossilised crinoids are in the outcrops beneath.

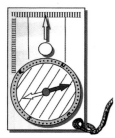

Route Walk up past the CP entrance and the first wood sculpture on the right, to join a path, right of an avenue of beech trees. This leads to a concessionary path, parallel to the **B6049** and sedately uphill, to emerge just before a road junction on the right to **Litton**. Head towards Litton, and take the first footpath on the right, uphill through a field, to meet a minor road. The path opposite first slants left and then right through fields and stiles to meet another minor road. Proceed ahead on this road for about a couple of hundred metres and take the track straight ahead as the road bears left. After about 250 metres, climb the wall stile on the right, (not too conspicuous, but it's just after a stile on the left). Over the stile, the path leads down and bears left into **Tansley Dale**. Short but florally rich, the dale descends into **Cressbrook Dale**, where stepping stones may be needed to cross a seasonal stream. Turn left, follow the path past **Peter's Stone** (go walkabout) and through a farmyard at **Wardlow Mires**. Turn right up the **B6465** to **Wardlow** and, just after the Bull's Head pub, but on the opposite side of the road, a footpath leads delightfully between walls to emerge high above Cressbrook Dale. Go on, and then straight ahead at a path junction. Soon, the path descends (rocky in places) to meet the path through the valley. Keep left, cross a footbridge, and immediately bear right, uphill (good views over

The florally rich flank of Cressbrook Dale is soon revealed from Wardlow (May 27)

to Ravensdale Crags) to a hairpin bend at a road. Continue up the road through **Cressbrook**, keep right, past the War Memorial on the right (so many fell from such a small hamlet), and straight ahead as a road joins from the left. About 250 metres on, take the path on the left, (views left to Water-cum-Jolly, Walk 41) which eventually zigzags downhill down to **Litton Mill**, where there is a fine race on the **R.Wye**. Turn right, and follow the pleasant riverside road along Miller's Dale for about 300 metres, to the entrance of **Tideswell Dale** on the right. Before starting up the dale, it is well worth continuing for another 300 metres to view **Ravenstor Crag**. If it's warm, there may be rock gymnasts performing. Back at the start of **Tideswell Dale**, steps lead up to the Youth Hostel, but we follow the valley floor and cross a footbridge at a junction to pass the "Ewe" and the "Owl" sculptures. But the most impressive carving is "The Quarryman", best reached by taking the track which leads up sharp right just before the car park. There are picnic tables up there, too.

40

Birchen, Gardom's and Baslow Edges via The Cundy Graves

Many stonemasons of old laid claim to rock by initialling it, but this work on Baslow Edge is unusual compared to others nearby (Sept 1)

As well as the scenery and rock formations, there is much more to see on this easy introduction to the Eastern Edges: The Three Ships and Nelson's Monument on Birchen Edge; The Eagle Stone and Wellington's Monument on Baslow Edge; a wildlife pond at Bar Brook; Neolithic rock art at Gardom's Edge and the haunting Cundy Graves.

Length 10 kms / 6.25 miles **Map** O/S Explorer OL 24, *White Peak Area*, East Sheet
Start/Finish Robin Hood Car Park east of Baslow off the B6050 at SK 280 721
Terrain Well-defined tracks and paths, some uphill. There is one short, marshy stretch.
Refreshments *Robin Hood Inn* next to the CP. Seasonal ice-cream van at Curbar Gap.
When To Go/What's There A walk for all seasons. The golden-ringed dragonfly, regionally rare, can be seen hawking up and down Bar Brook late June/early July. Water voles and plants such as marsh violet, marsh pennywort and northern marsh orchid can be seen at the brook. A plant rare in The Peak, navelwort, is occasionally seen on gritstone walls beneath Baslow Edge. Here, lie the poignant graves of the Cundy family who, it is said, succumbed to the plague 34 years before it hit Eyam. Another sad memorial is the *Three Men* - 3 stone cairns on Gardom's Edge, allegedly to 3 travellers who perished one winter long ago. A few yards away lies a prehistoric settlement with rock art (photo p.18), a standing stone and dwelling remains. The *Three Ships* are rocks carved with the names of Nelson's flagships, one incorrectly. His monument provides the best belay for climbers! There is a guide stoop en route to *Wellington's Monument* and a toposcope at the end of Baslow Edge. The old mill pond at Bar Brook has matured into an important wetland habitat. The walk is most striking when the heather blooms. There is a boulder engraved *JG 1816* (see map) and others with biblical quotations (see *Route*). **Nearby** are Shillito Wood cross and a stone circle at SK 278 755. See p.241 for suggested route.

From this aspect, The Eagle Stone on Baslow Edge looks more like a frog (May 25). In times past, the young men of Baslow had to prove their manhood by ascending the rock prior to their engagement. It's a tricky ascent, but at least the landing is fairly soft!

Bar Brook mill pond with the start of Gardom's Edge top left of picture (Sept 1)

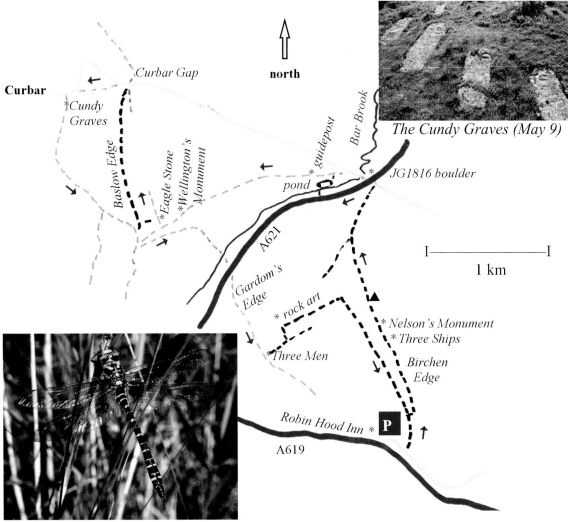

Curbar Gap

north

Curbar

Cundy Graves

Baslow Edge

*Eagle Stone

*Wellington's Monument

guidepost

Bar Brook

pond

A621

* JG1816 boulder

The Cundy Graves (May 9)

1 km

Gardom's Edge

* rock art

* Nelson's Monument
* Three Ships

*Three Men

Birchen Edge

Robin Hood Inn * P

A619

Male golden-ringed dragonfly at Bar Brook (June 28)

Approaching the Three Ships with a group already at Nelson's Monument (Dec 23)

Route Turn left out of the CP and, after 40m, go left at a gate/stile. About 200m up the path, at a bench-marked boulder on the left, turn right up the path which rises steeply to the top of **Birchen Edge**. Here, turn left to reach the **Three Ships** and **Nelson's Monument**. Just before the trig point, a narrow gully leads down to a path. Turn right and head north through a marshy section to a ladder stile, at a minor road near to the **A621**. Cross the A621 (**JG1816 boulder**, see map) and turn left down the footpath for about 200m, to where a grassed-over bridge crosses **Bar Brook** to a **pond**. From the pond, a path leads up to a track. Go left, and pass the *Chesterfeild Roade* **guidepost** to the cross of **Wellington's Monument** (seat). Bear right to the conspicuous **Eagle Stone**. Now, walk west (left) off-track for about 80m and turn right on the path which runs along the top of **Baslow Edge** (not the main path) to reach **Curbar Gap**. Take the left gate, walk down the road a few metres and go left at the stile (NT sign *Curbar Gap* after boulders inscribed to *Hebrews* and *Isaiah*) and walk down through fields/stiles to the road. After a few metres, take the stile on the left (then an awkward gate) to the **Cundy Graves**. Onwards, after a green metal gate, the path bears left uphill to path junctions. Stay right until a gate with two large boulders is reached. Don't go through, but turn 90° left on a path that clings to the left of a wall, enters oak woodland and veers right, downhill, past an interesting dwelling and over Bar Brook to the A621. Cross the road, and a path leads up woodland to a wall and gate posts at the end of **Gardom's Edge**. Turn left up the path to the left of the wall to reach a narrow gateless opening and the cairns of the **Three Men**. Go over the stile on the right just before the cairns. The path forks after about 140m. Go left to ancient settlement remains and an old wall. Follow wall to its end. 50m beyond and to the right, is the **rock art**. From here, a faint path leads towards Birchen Edge and, at a wall corner, meets the path that runs beneath the edge. Turn right and follow the path back down to the B6050.

Curbar Edge from the road to the Cundy Graves (March 23)

41

Monsal Dale, High Dale and Water-cum-Jolly High Route

The weir in Monsal Dale in full spate (Sept 23)

This most scenic of walks starts at the Monsal Head viewpoint; descends to Hobs House for flowers and fossils; circuits a photogenic weir on The Wye and rises to the track to Brushfield and an aerial view of Monsal Dale that no camera could do justice to. High Dale leads to Priestcliffe Lees nature reserve, but the pièce de résistance is a scintillating traverse high above Water-cum-Jolly on the relict railman's Plate-layers' Path.

Length 11 kms / 6.9 miles **Map** O/S Explorer OL 24, *White Peak Area*, East Sheet
Start/Finish Monsal Head (SK 184 715) : pay CP or free roadside (to Little Longstone)
Terrain Easy to follow tracks and paths, but those above Water-cum-Jolly must be taken with care as there are drops that could be fatal. Watch the kids/pets and go sober! Also, if you visit Hobs House (optional) do not climb the loose pinnacles or enter the "cave".
Refreshments Pub, café, restaurant and ice-cream van at Monsal Head.
When To Go/What's There The scenery is wonderful throughout the year and little grebe, tufted duck, swan, dipper and goosander are resident on The Wye. In spring, lily-of-the-valley, violets, spearwort, water avens, and, if its damp, slow-worms are on the path to the weir, and the riverside is ablaze with marsh marigolds. Later, Hobs House has Jacob's-ladder and crosswort. It is an SSSI for fossils (p.17), and the walls to Brushfield display crinoids. The high flanks of Monsal Dale have abundant rock-rose, birds-foot trefoil and thyme, and these and other plants attract northern brown argus, dingy skipper and common blue butterflies, to name three of ten. High Dale has a colony of black rabbits. Priestcliffe Lees also has spring sandwort, yellow rattle, profuse wood anemones, orchids, and the oddly named grass-of-Parnassus, also found late summer above Water-cum-Jolly. The birdsong in Monsal Dale is a joy in spring. **Nearby** Longstone Moor has footpaths over this precious but threatened gem, where heather blooms on the limestone heath; skylarks sing above the mountain pansies and lizards bask in the sun (SK 19-73-).

Monsal Dale, with rock-rose in the foreground and Hobs House upper right. Taken from Monsal Head Crags, on access land via a gate on the B6465 (June 28).

Springtime on the Plate-layers' Path, high above Water-cum-Jolly (May 18)

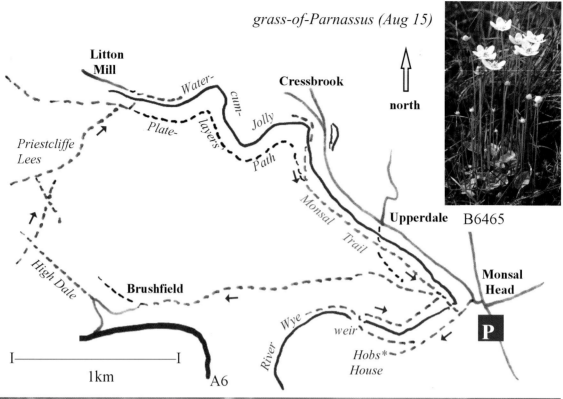

grass-of-Parnassus (Aug 15)

north

Litton Mill

Water-cum-

Jolly

Cressbrook

Plate-

layers'

Priestcliffe Lees

Path

Monsal Trail

Upperdale B6465

High Dale

Brushfield

Monsal Head

P

River Wye

weir

Hobs* House

1km

A6

An astonishing display of common dog-violets at the bottom of High Dale (April 19)
Inset. *Moorhen's nest beside the River Wye in Monsal Dale (April 19)*

Route Take the minor road right of the Monsal Head Hotel. A few metres past the café on the left, go through an opening in the wall ahead and turn left on the path signed to *Monsal Dale* and *Ashford*. The path soon forks left to Ashford, so remain on the path which leads down into the valley. If you wish to visit **Hobs House**, after some "root steps" and, about 100m above the river below, a narrow path leads left off the main path, through trees and onto a grassy bank to the limestone outcrops, where it is stony underfoot and there are loose blocks. Return by the same way and descend to the **weir**, cross the footbridge ahead and turn right, passing the weir on the **River Wye** again. Just before the viaduct, take one of the paths that run left, uphill to a gate to the Monsal Trail. Don't go through the gate but go left up the stony footpath which leads to a track coming up from **Upperdale**. At the top, opposite a dew pond and small standing stone, walk out left for the view. The track and way ahead leads through gates to the hamlet of **Brushfield**, where it joins a road. Turn left down the road and leave it on the right at a hairpin bend (4 ancient troughs over fence, right). Go over the stile (ignore access land gate, right) and up **High Dale**. Where the wall on the right turns 90° right, you do also up a shallow valley and over fields to a track. Turn left, pass a footpath sign on the right until a stile and entrance to **Priestcliffe Lees** Nature Reserve is reached. Follow the path across the spoil heaps and all the way downhill to where steps lead down to the Monsal Trail at a bridge. Go right and along the trail, pass some misleading signs until a sealed tunnel entrance is reached. Go up the path to the left of the tunnel to a stile. As the narrow paths ahead fork, always keep right and uphill to where the **Plate-layers' Path** levels out at some shallow caves on the right. The way ahead now undulates past some spectacular scenery as the River Wye far below meanders through the limestone gorge of **Water-cum-Jolly**. You will also see a lower path above the gorge, but for a first time it is best to follow this higher path until it eventually swings right and descends to a path which leads to the **Monsal Trail** again. Turn left on the trail and follow it past the old station platform and over the viaduct (good views up and down the River Wye) to the path which leads uphill to **Monsal Head** again.

The crumbling towers at Hobs House (May 31). Tread very gingerly if you visit the site.

42 | Great Shacklow Wood, Deep Dale and The Magpie Mine

A wintry scene at Fere Mere in Monyash (Jan 20)

This walk with interest in both natural and industrial history starts at the Sheepwash Bridge in Ashford; follows the River Wye to an old bobbin mill and the sough (drainage outlet) to the Magpie Mine; meanders up and down Great Shacklow Wood; rises up the floral riches of Deep Dale and visits popular Monyash, the Magpie Mine and Sheldon.

Length 15 kms / 9.4 miles **Map** O/S Explorer OL 24, *White Peak Area*, East Sheet
Start/Finish Sheepwash Bridge, Ashford, SK 194 695. There is a car park in the village.
Terrain A long but easy walk on paths, tracks and minor roads. A few gentle rises.
Refreshments Pub, café at Monyash; pub at Sheldon; pubs and shop at Ashford
When To Go/What's There Anytime, but the walk comes alive in early and late spring when the wildlife awakens. Water voles and marsh marigolds appear beside The Wye, which also supports dipper, little grebe and tufted duck. Trout leap for flies above pools stalked by herons. Toothwort, bluebell, ramson, dog's mercury, wood sorrel, red campion, arum lily and water aven highlight Great Shacklow Wood. As you exit, violet, primrose and a carpet of wood anemone greet you. Deep Dale is a symphony of cowslips, with oxlip, columbine, meadow saxifrage and early purple orchid. Skylark, curlew, kestrel and wheatear perform over paradoxical High Low, where an information board is beside a dew pond supporting newts, frogs, whirligig beetles and damselflies. The Magpie Mine has interesting relics, three colour forms of mountain pansy and spring sandwort. Fere Mere at Monyash, the sole survivor of four local meres (p.33), has brown hawker and broad-bodied dragonflies and yellow flag. The atmospheric bobbin mill before Great Shacklow Wood has been the location for a number of films, but the twin waterwheels are rapidly degrading (photo). **Nearby** Ashford-in-the-Water itself is worth a few minutes and even longer at well dressing time (dates in *Peak District* annual paper). You can also stroll beside the River Wye south of the village to see the swans.

Approaching the Magpie Mine (May 9). **Inset.** *Two of the three colour forms of mountain pansy found here (May 9). Spring sandwort also flourishes on the spoil heaps.*

Cowslip time in Deep Dale (May 7). Millions flower here. **Inset.** *Toothwort is parasitic on the roots of beech trees in Great Shacklow Wood (April 22)*

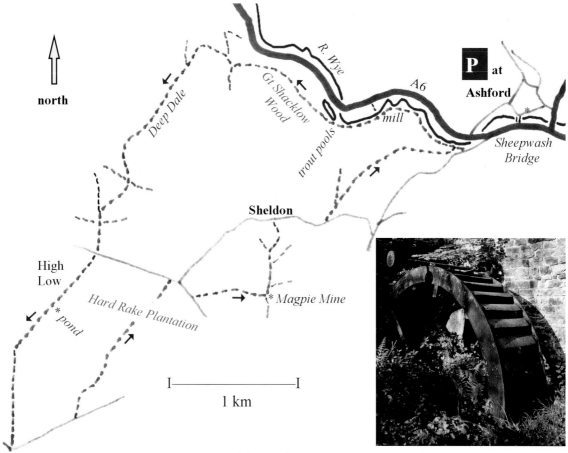

One of the two waterwheels at the old bobbin mill (May 9)

Ramsons beside the path through Great Shacklow Wood (May 9)

Route From **Ashford**, cross the river via the **Sheepwash Bridge**. Cross the **A6** and turn right. Walk up the pavement and turn left up the minor road signposted to Sheldon. After about 200m, turn right and along the path beside the **River Wye**. Follow this to the bobbin **mill**; pass the sough which drains the mine 2 kms above; pause at the **trout pools**, then undulate through **Great Shacklow Wood**. As you exit the wood, go through a gate. Further on, keep left at the path junctions to arrive at the bottom of **Deep Dale**. Follow the path all the way up the dale until it merges with a track. Turn left up the track to a road. Cross the road and walk up the walled path over **High Low**. The path then enters open fields and, after a small wood on the right, veers to the left over stiles and fields to a road. If you wish to visit **Monyash** it is straight ahead, but the route turns left along the road for about ½ km and turns left again to enter more farmland. Head for the left corner of the first field and the way ahead follows more stiles and fields. As you near **Hard Rake Plantation**, keep the wall on the left, despite one confusingly positioned stile. After the plantation, the path reaches a road. Turn right, keep ahead at the left junction and turn left off the road after about 150m. Over the stile, the path crosses fields and fallen walls to your visible quarry - the **Magpie Mine**. From the tall, round chimney, two paths lead in a northerly direction. Take the left path to a stile and cross fields to a track. Cross the track and go through more fields and stiles to **Sheldon**. Turn right, down the road (pub on right) to the last dwelling on the left (Lower Farm). A few metres past, go through the gate on the left. Soon the path forks. Go right (don't enter wood) and the path soon becomes a view-filled descent to the River Wye, where you retrace your steps to Ashford-in-the-Water.

River water-crowfoot flowering in the River Wye at the Sheepwash Bridge (June 28)

43

Chatsworth, Dobb Edge, The Jubilee Rock and Edensor

Chatsworth House and Park in the autumn (Oct 31)

A walk which visits the splendour of Chatsworth House; the whimsical architecture of the village of Edensor; the Jubilee Rock (inscribed to commemorate Queen Victoria's 1887 golden jubilee); The Grotto with its follies and water features (or the Emperor and Swiss Lakes) and the views from Dobb Edge and the Rabbit Warren. To its great credit, the estate adopts a relaxed attitude to visitors, who are free to roam over much of the park.

Length 12 kms / 7.5 miles **Map** O/S Explorer OL 24, *White Peak Area*, East Sheet
Start/Finish Calton Lees car park between Edensor and Beeley at SK 258 685 (P&D)
Terrain An easy walk on tracks and paths. All the uphill work is at the start of the walk.
Refreshments Courtyard Restaurant/bar/self-service at Chatsworth; tea rooms Edensor.
When To Go/What's There If you opt to visit Chatsworth House as part of your visit, take a change of footwear. The House and Gardens normally close for winter, but there are exceptions at Xmas time. Deer can be seen throughout the year in their many forms. Buzzards, once a rare sight in The Peak, now breed in the woods and are frequently observed. Sparrow-hawk, kestrel, merlin, goshawk and hobby top up the raptors, the latter most often appearing when there is a glut of northern eggar moths on nearby Beeley Moor. Skylarks sing above the Rabbit Warren, and an occasional snipe, woodcock or brown hare may appear. All three British woodpeckers are here and nest boxes in the woods are used by avian visitors, including pied flycatcher. The lakes support teal; The Derwent tufted duck and goosander and two ponds six species of dragonfly. The Grotto has ornamental waterfalls and aqueducts; the Hunting Tower three cannon; and woods in *ER* logo can (to date) be seen from Dobb Edge, which has a pinnacle and millstones.
Nearby is a fine guide stoop on Beeley Moor (SK 295 673), but *Hob Hurst's House* is basically a crater. Baslow is worth a peep for its unusual church clock face (*VICTORIA 1897*) and the tiny toll guard house on the ancient bridge over the River Derwent.

Top. *Fallow deer stags and Edensor church steeple (Oct 12).* **Inset.** *Part of the inscription on Jubilee Rock.* **Bottom.** *Chatsworth Park in winter (Dec 29).* **Inset.** *Architectural fun at Edensor. Every dwelling has a different design.*

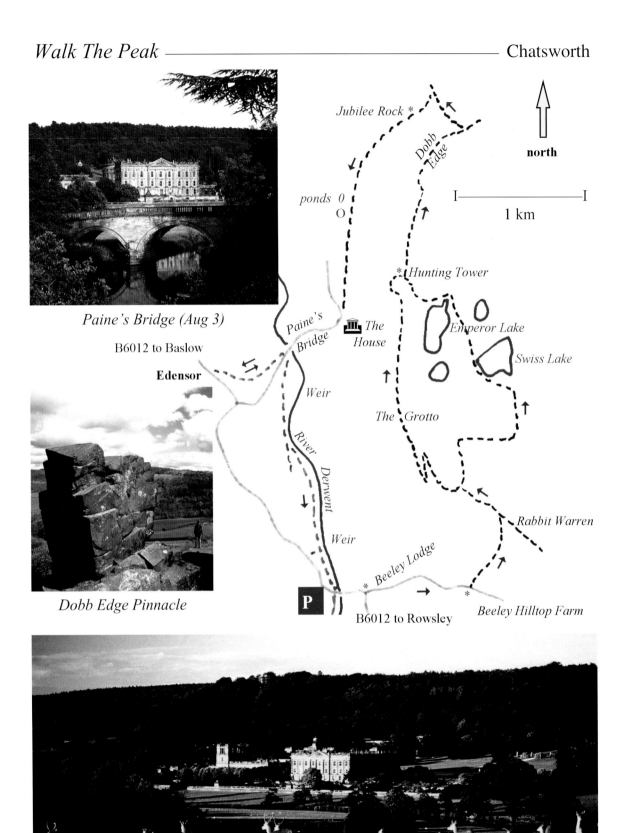

Paine's Bridge (Aug 3)

B6012 to Baslow

Edensor

Dobb Edge Pinnacle

Jubilee Rock *

Dobb Edge

ponds 0
       O

1 km

north

* *Hunting Tower*

Emperor Lake

Paine's Bridge

The House

Swiss Lake

Weir

The Grotto

River Derwent

Weir

Rabbit Warren

Beeley Lodge

P

B6012 to Rowsley

* *Beeley Hilltop Farm*

Red deer and Chatsworth House, with the Hunting Tower just visible above (July 28)

Route From the car park, cross the road and walk down to the **River Derwent**. Turn right and follow the path downstream until a gate is reached at a bridge. Go left over the bridge and stay on the **B6012** for about 100 m, then go up the minor road at **Beeley Lodge**. Leave this at **Beeley Hilltop Farm** by taking the footpath opposite, which climbs gently up to the **Rabbit Warren**. Here, there are extensive views of the lower Derwent Valley. Bear left to a wall stile and enter the woods where the main track soon forks to go (a) left downhill to **The Grotto** with its water features, or (b) right to meander beside the lakes (the **Emperor Lake** is the header tank for the fountain in the formal gardens). Both routes lead to the **Hunting Tower**, but if you go via The Grotto, take the right, uphill tracks/paths after. From the tower, a track leads onwards through woods before turning left after a farm on the right to reach a wall stile. Over, bear left to walk above the bays of **Dobb Edge** to the pinnacle and wall stile ahead. Do not climb it, but walk left, down the bendy track until it ends after about 100m and you enter parkland opposite a gate in the wall on the right. To find the **Jubilee Rock**, now set your compass to 280° and angle down left for about 300m. The rock appears as a lumpy boulder in front of oaks and about 200m above a track that runs through the park. From the rock, head south then angle right to reach the track which passes horse trials obstacles and two fine wildlife **ponds** en route to **Chatsworth House**. Cross **Paine's Bridge** over The Derwent and take the path rising right, to the village of **Edensor**. Return to the bridge and follow the riverside path downstream. Just after the second **weir** (where in autumn trout leap), ascend right to reach the road and car park.

Ice trees (a rare phenomenon, courtesy of freezing fog) on the path to Edensor (Jan 1).
Inset. *Chatsworth House reflected in the River Derwent (July 28).*

44

Bradford Dale, Alport and Lathkill Dale National Nature Reserve

Looking down on walkers in Lathkill Dale from one of the vantage points (June 5)

This limestone scenery outing starts from the picturesque hamlet of Alport; rises to give an aerial view of Bradford Dale, before descending to journey through the upper part of the dale with its weirs, trout pools and associated wildlife; rises on a stretch of the "Limestone Way" to the medieval farm of One Ash Grange and then descends into Lathkill Dale for a ramble through this precious National Nature Reserve in its entirety.

Length 16 kms / 10 miles **Map** O/S Explorer OL 24, *White Peak Area*, East Sheet
Start/Finish Lay-bys near the phone box in Alport, 1km E of Youlgreave, SK 219 645
Terrain A fairly long walk but most paths are good. There are stony sections which have to be taken with care in slippery conditions. Farm fields may be muddy. Some roadwork.
Refreshments Tea rooms in Bradford Dale; *Lathkill Head Hotel* (uphill detour, see map)
When To Go/What's There A fine walk whatever time of the year, but best between April and September. Bats emanate from a fissure high in Parsons Crag late afternoon, and raptors occasionally try to catch them. The bats invariably perform a lazy somersault and the birds flash past empty-clawed! Mosses and liverworts extract calcium from the water and form tufa, best observed at the only natural waterfall in Lathkill Dale. The pools have water-starwort, water-crowfoot and fool's water-cress. Green hellibore, brown marsh sedge and yellow star-of-Bethlehem are local rarities. The flowers attract many butterflies and hoverflies. There are wheatears, lapwings, dippers, grey wagtails and herons, and the air is alive with warblers' songs in spring. Huge trout can be seen from Raper Bridge, which has florally-cocooned weirs. There are fine stands of Jacob's-ladder in upper Lathkill Dale (end June). Look out for the medieval pigsties at One Ash Grange. Don't enter Lathkill Head Cave (the true source of The Lathkill) or any of the mines (especially The Mandale Mine), as they are prone to instant flooding, even when the river appears dry.
Nearby Arbor Low henge (p.19) is a must at SK 160 635 (signs on A515).

Top Left. *Parson's Crag supports stonecrop, mullein and several species of geranium on the scree, and thyme and hawkweeds on the flanks.* **Top Right.** *The tufa waterfall is the only natural cascade on the River Lathkill (both June 26).* **Bottom.** *Looking down on the riverside path from above Conksbury Bridge (May 1).*

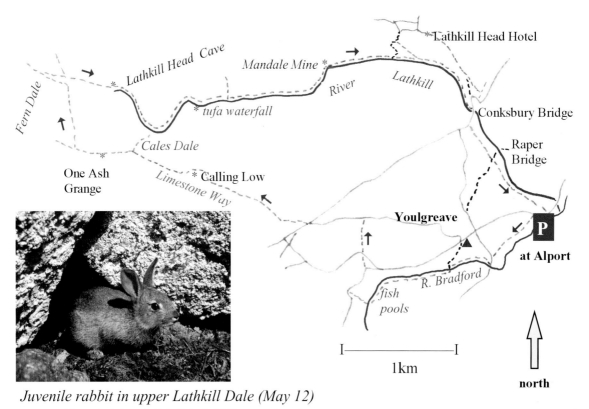

Juvenile rabbit in upper Lathkill Dale (May 12)

Passing one of the weirs in Bradford Dale (June 5). The river has, of late, less water.

Route Walk uphill on the footpath for about 50 metres, then go through the stile on the left. Follow the path through fields above the **River Bradford** to a road. Turn left, downhill, and soon right to engage the path beside the right bank of the river. Continue upstream to a footbridge. Cross the river and walk up the left bank; pass a series of **fish pools** (little grebes), and then cross the river over a bridge, noting the motto on the coping stones. A path leads (right fork) uphill to a road. Turn right. After about 400 metres, take the first footpath on the left, uphill to another minor road. Across the road is a stile which leads through fields and stiles to another minor road. Go left up the road. After about 600 metres, pass a picnic site on the left and, just after, join another road. Go over the stile on the right, signposted ***The Limestone Way***. The path crosses fields and stiles to by-pass **Calling Low Farm**, and later descends via steep steps into **Cales Dale**. Keep ahead, uphill at a path junction to pass through the medieval farm of **One Ash Grange**. After about 300 metres, turn 90° right off the track, and take the path which eventually swings left to join **Lathkill Dale** at the beginning of the short **Fern Dale**. Turn right, and follow the path past **Lathkill Head Cave** to a footbridge on the right. Opposite this, a path leads uphill to views to the left and right (optional). Return to the valley. Later, the way downstream enters ash woodland and passes the **Mandale Mine** ruins before reaching a dwelling. Here, stay on the left bank as the river widens out to reach **Conksbury Bridge**. (From here, a short detour uphill leads to a stile and an aerial view, photo). Whatever, turn right at the bridge over the **River Lathkill,** and then turn first left through fields (short detour left to **Raper Bridge**, weir etc., recommended), and follow the riverside path back to the **Alport** lay-by.

On the path through the upper reaches of Lathkill Dale (May 11).
Inset. *One of dozens of dark mullein plants that grow here (June 22).*

45 Peak Tor, Stanton in Peak and Haddon Hall

Beech trees in autumn on the summit of Peak Tor (Oct 25). In the spring, there are carpets of bluebells beneath the trees. There is more to Peak Tor than is documented.

No visit to the Peak District is complete without a visit to its most beautiful medieval manor house - Haddon Hall. Our walk also encompasses the earthwork on the flanks of Peak Tor; the conservation village of Stanton in Peak and stretches of the River Wye.

Length 12 kms/7.5 miles **Map** O/S Explorer OL 24, *White Peak Area*, East Sheet
Start/Finish Caudwells Mill car park at Rowsley, off the A6 at SK 256 657
Terrain Paths and tracks, some of which can be muddy after heavy rain. So if you intend to visit Haddon Hall, take change of footwear. Some roadwork: narrow/pathless.
Refreshments Café at Haddon Hall and Caudwells Mill. Pubs at Rowsley and Stanton.
When To Go/What's There The ideal time is during Rowsley well-dressings at the end of June, when the roses also bloom at Haddon Hall and, if it's a sunny day, broad-bodied chaser dragonflies will be on the wing at the dew pond above Shiningbank Quarry. Wild flowers along the way may include biting stonecrop, burdock, creeping cinquefoil, hawkweeds, clovers, oxeye daisy and bird's-foot trefoil. The dew pond has curled pondweed; the River Wye supports river water-crowfoot, yellow flag, water voles, little grebes, dippers and kingfishers. The plaintive call of the lapwing can be heard over the fields, and martins and raptors nest on the worked-out limestone faces of Shiningbank Quarry. Buzzards soar above The Wye Valley and nest locally. There is a unique roadside belvedere on the way to Stanton, with views to Haddon. The earthwork we follow below Peak Tor is thought to be an Anglo-Danish park pale (enclosure). There is a similar earth bank across the river in fields above Rowsley, not referred to. Whatever the season, the walk is both atmospheric and interesting. Start early and leave a little time to visit Caudwells Mill, where flour is ground as of old. Buy some! **Nearby** Peak Outlets retail park at Rowsley has a couple of outdoor clothing shops, should you be in need of a fix.

Haddon Hall is best visited when the roses bloom (June 24). It closes for winter.

Peak Tor seen from the River Wye at Rowsley. The earthwork is just visible beneath the beech-crowned hill. The trout weir on the river is man-made (May 23).

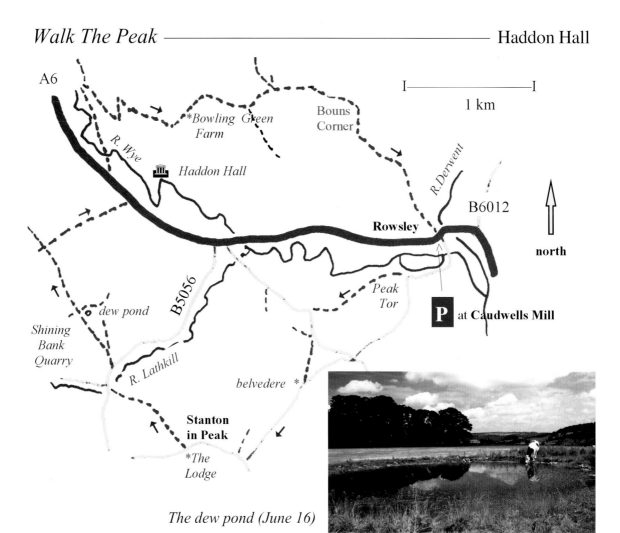

A6

R. Wye

Bowling Green Farm

Bouns Corner

R.Derwent

Haddon Hall

B6012

Rowsley

1 km

north

B5056

dew pond

Peak Tor

Shining Bank Quarry

P at **Caudwells Mill**

R. Lathkill

belvedere *

Stanton in Peak

*The Lodge

The dew pond (June 16)

Films shot at Haddon Hall include "The Princess Bride" and "Jane Eyre".

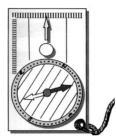

Route Turn right out of the car park, cross the bridge over the **River Wye** on the road and, after about 200m, take the signed footpath on the right. This leads to the earthwork on **Peak Tor**, which is followed until the embankment swings left. Here, keep straight on to the right end of a small wood where stiles/gates lead to a minor road. Turn left up the narrow lane and take the second footpath on the right, which leads up fields to another road and the **belvedere**. Turn right and follow the road to **Stanton in Peak** keeping right at a road junction. Pass the church and war memorial on the left (seats). After the Flying Childers pub, walk down the road out of the village. Opposite **The Lodge** a footpath heads across a field to the left corner, where it bears left down an avenue of ancient red hawthorns and onwards to steps down through a short wood to the **B5056**. Turn right, cross the **River Lathkill** and the road and take the track ahead, uphill, passing an aerial view of Shiningbank

Well dressing at Rowsley (June 24). Note the carved and dated coronet above the well. We see more stone coronets on Walk 46.

Quarry down to the left. Opposite the end of the quarry face, a stile on the right leads to the wildlife dewpond. Following a peep, return to the track and ahead it soon enters old and new woodland. After the woods the path reaches a X-path junction where you turn right to eventually reach the **A6**. Cross the road: ahead is the entrance to **Haddon Hall** if you're visiting, but the route itself turns left up the footpath for about 250m, until an inconspicuous stile in the wall on the right is reached. The path now leads between fences for a short distance; crosses The Wye and soon opens out to run beside the river to a track. A short distance left is a footbridge and a good place to look for kingfishers, but the route turns right up the track, passes over the entrance to Haddon railway tunnel, before being directed off the track and on to a path on the right. Across fields the path joins another track at **Bowling Green Farm** and this is followed, avoiding a track on the right, until a view of an unexpected valley is seen on the left. Further on, keep right at a track junction and this track eventually falls through woodland at **Bouns Corner** and tumbles down through old **Rowsley** to the A6. Here, beside the beautiful Peacock Hotel, is the well and coronet.

Stanton Moor, Rowtor Rocks and Robin Hood's Stride

Robin Hood's Stride is known locally as Mock Beggars' Hall (June 21)

As well as outstanding natural rock formations, the grits of the Birchover and Stanton in Peak areas are also rich in carvings, engravings and Neolithic remains. Allow a full day to find and see all that this most interesting walk has to offer. Take a torch each, too!

Length 12 kms / 7.5 miles **Map** O/S Explorer OL 24, *White Peak Area*, East Sheet
Start/Finish Roadside parking on the B5056, a few metres north of the prominent gravel track which leads up to Robin Hood's Stride. SK 228 618. Restricted spaces, go early.
Terrain Sandy paths, tracks and farmland paths. A little roadwork. A few gentle uphill sections. Potentially dangerous drops from Rowtor Rocks and Robin Hood's Stride.
Refreshments *Druids Inn*, *Red Lion Inn* and shop at Birchover. Also conveniences.
When To Go/What's There The walk starts with a visit to the gated *Hermit's Cave* (torch) to see the carved crucifix, niche and external carved guttering - now a hand-traverse for rock-climbers! The graffiti and views from *Robin Hood's Stride* are followed by *Nine Stones Circle* (p.19). *Rowtor Rocks* hold a 300 year-old labyrinth of steps, rooms (torch), alcoves and even armchairs, all carved by the Rev. Thomas Eyre of Birchover. The *Andle Stone* sports iron rungs (1758) to the summit graffiti, but the real gem hides behind the rock, where there is an exquisitely carved commemoration to local landowner Col. William Thornhill and Wellington. On Stanton Moor, the *Cork Stone* (rungs) leads to the over-popular *Nine Ladies* stone circle which, in turn, leads to Stanton Moor Edge. Here, there is a boulder carved with a coronet and a Y (1826); a coronet with G (1854) and stonemason's initials (AGEN); the *Earl Grey Tower*; the *Cat Stone* (EIN 1831) and, soon after, the oldest graffiti (DR 1615) on a path-side boulder. Upper Town reveals stocks and, further on, a ruin has niches, carvings and an ancient trough. Wildlife includes mining bees, cuckoo, skylark, kestrel, southern hawker dragonfly, bilberry, greater bellflower, foxglove, wood sage, harebell, and fungi. Silver birch and bracken are ousting heather on Stanton Moor. **Nearby** *Doll Tor* circle is in a wood at SK 238 628.

Top Left. *The 1826 coronet on Stanton Moor Edge was carved on an isolated boulder to celebrate the Duke of York. Nearby, is the 1854 coronet.* **Top Right.** *The carved graffiti on the weathered pinnacle at Robin Hood's Stride.* **Bottom Left.** *Approaching Lion Rock from the carved armchairs at Rowtor Rocks. Behind and below the armchairs is a rock with faint cup and ring markings, best seen when wet.* **Bottom Right.** *Stocks at Upper Town, Birchover, restored in 1951. Local archaeological finds are now in Sheffield's Weston Park Museum.*

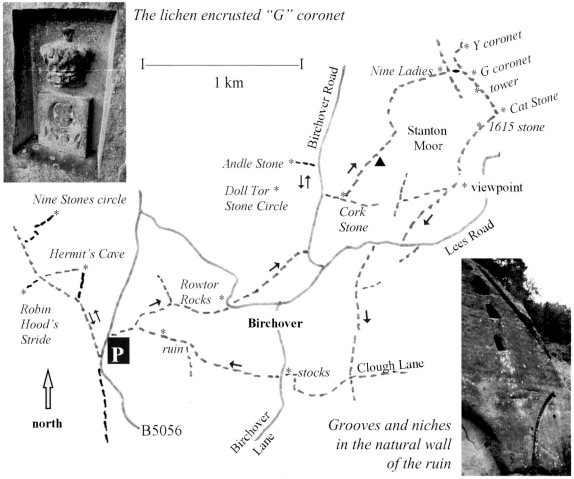

The lichen encrusted "G" coronet

I——————————————I
1 km

Y coronet

Nine Ladies   *G coronet*

tower

Cat Stone

1615 stone

Stanton
Moor

Andle Stone

viewpoint

Doll Tor
Stone Circle

Birchover Road

Cork
Stone

Lees Road

Nine Stones circle

Hermit's Cave

Rowtor
Rocks

Birchover

*Robin
Hood's
Stride*

P

ruin

stocks   Clough Lane

north

B5056   Birchover Lane

*Grooves and niches
in the natural wall
of the ruin*

*The archaeological dig at Nine Ladies stone circle in 2000 was commissioned by English
Heritage and undertaken by the Trent and Peak Archaeological Society (Nov 19).*

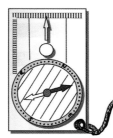

Route Cross the **B5056**, go over the stile and walk up the conspicuous gravel track towards **Robin Hood's Stride**. As the track bears right to Cratcliff Cottage, keep ahead until you see a wall stile to the right of the main path. This leads up through the wood to the **Hermit's Cave**, which is below the crag beside two mature yew trees. Either return to the main path or ascend left to a path across fields to reach Robin Hood's Stride, best ascended around the right pinnacle. **Nine Stones** circle can be seen to the north and is reached by leaving the footpath ahead via gates and fields. Return to the B5056, turn left, cross the road and, after about 100 m, take the path uphill to a track. Turn left and, just before the Druids Inn, a narrow entrance in a wall on the left leads up to the lower tier of **Rowtor Rocks**. Steps in a cleft (room on right) lead to the upper level. Return to the lane, pass the Druids, cross the road and, beside the Millennium Stone, a path leads up through woods to **Birchover Road**. Turn left, follow road for about ½ km until level with the **Andle Stone**, situated 100 metres across a field on the left. A gate gives access to the field. Return to road, turn right. After about 200 m, turn left to where a stile and then sandy path leads to the **Cork Stone**. Turn left then right at the fork. Pass the trig pillar and bear left at the main path to **Nine Ladies** circle. Here, turn right (bearing 70°) to a stile at a fence, about 50 metres away. (Be careful to select the correct path, take compass). Go over, turn left to the **Y coronet**, 200 metres ahead on the right. Return, pass stile, and the **G coronet** is about 100 m ahead, a little off the path on the left. Onwards leads to the **tower**. Stay on same path to the **Cat Stone**, situated where the path turns 90° right. Soon after, the **1615** boulder is on the right. The path reaches a stile on the right. To the left is a **viewpoint** rock. Pass the stile and descend to **Lees Road**. Turn right and soon left off the road on to a path which leads through Barn Farm (peacocks) and across farm fields to a track (**Clough Lane**) at a X-junction. Here, turn right and follow the lane past Uppertown Farm (emu and ostrich) to the stocks. To the left of the **stocks**, a footpath leads through a field (avoid 5-bar gate on left) to a footpath gate. Onwards, the path joins another at a dwelling then reaches a small **ruin** on the right (photo p.222) and, ahead, the point where you ascended to from the B5056. Goldcrests are seen in the pines here. Now descend to the car parking area.

From one aspect, The Cork Stone resembles a champagne cork (Sept 7)

47 Long Dale, Gratton Dale and Kenslow Knoll

The bottom of Long Dale where, **Inset***, the dark green fritillary is abundant (July 13)*

As well as visiting the floral displays in Long Dale and Gratton Dale, this longish but not too taxing walk delivers interesting rock outcrops, sculptures and several fine views.

Length 14 kms/8.75 miles **Map** O/S Explorer OL 24, *White Peak Area*, East Sheet
Start/Finish Friden Car Park on the High Peak Trail (off the A5012 at SK 171 607)
Terrain Mainly farmland paths and tracks with some road sections. A few gentle rises.
Refreshments None on route. Elton (1 km round detour) has weekend café and pub.
When To Go/What's There After heavy rain, Gratton Dale can be very muddy and flooded at the end of the dale. In spring, the approaches to Long Dale have snowdrops, cowslips and orchids but some flowers among the dolomite limestone rocks in the dale are smaller than those in Gratton Dale due to sheep grazing. These include dropwort, gentian, hawkweeds, kidney vetch, saw-wort and mountain St John's-wort. Stemless thistle needs no grazing. In summer, the herb-rich grasslands attract common blue, dingy skipper, small copper, meadow brown and the conspicuous, but oddly named, dark green fritillary butterfly. Gratton Dale, too, has interest with globeflower, spleenwort, mountain everlasting and the more noticeable rock rose, thyme, scabious, knapweed, yellow rattle and ox-eye daisy. At the bottom of the dale is an old lime kiln. Other plants include tufted vetch, harebell, gorse and foxglove. There are rabbits, brown hares, weasels and birds such as wheatear, lapwing, skylark, partridge, buzzard, redstart and spotted flycatcher. A vestigial alter with crosses and etched lines are in a crag "cave" near Rock House. Look out for *The Triptych*, *Peace Stone* and other sculptures on the way to the human sundial on Kenslow Knoll. To date, there are "llamas" at Rock Farm and the trough beside the seat on Cliff Lane has freshwater shrimps and curled pondweed. Long Dale exibits much sheep terracing on the south-west side. **Nearby** and only a short drive after the walk is the fabulous *"Blake's Boulder"*. It sits beside a minor road at SK 200 616. Photo p.226.

Top. *If the sun is out and you know what month it is (sorry), you can determine the time on the human sundial at Kenslow Knoll (Nov 3).*

Left. *The Triptych in the bottom of Long Dale is one of a number of uplifting sculptures seen on route (July 13).*

Right. *"The Peace Of Running Water To You" stone lies seductively in Rowlow Brook on the way to Weaddow Lane (July 13).*

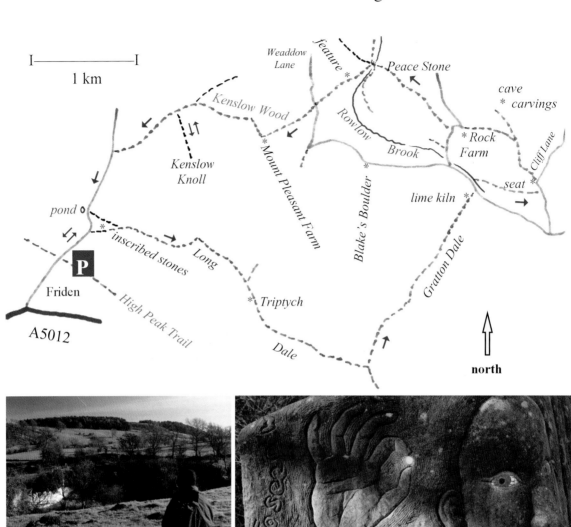

Top Left. *Reading the inscription on the circular stone feature.*
Top Right. *Part of the exquisite sculpturing on "Blake's Boulder". The inscribed words are from William Blake's "Auguries of Innocence" : "To see a World in a Grain of Sand, And Heaven in a Wild Flower, Hold Infinity in the palm of your hand, And Eternity in an hour". The carvings are on five faces of the cube-shaped boulder.*
Bottom Right. *One of the pair of "The Road Up And ..." stones.*

Route Turn right out of the car park entrance and walk down the road. After about 400 m, a path runs through the verge on the right down to a gate. Pass through and the way runs between walls (pair of **inscribed stones** after 100 m) before open land. After the plantation on the left, the path turns 90° left and uphill to a gate. (Optional route through bottom of dale). The way now runs above **Long Dale**. When a footpath joins from the left, the route slants right, to the dale bottom and the **Triptych**. Here, go through the gate. Further on there is now access to nature reserve on right. At the end of the dale a gate on the left is the entrance to **Gratton Dale**. At the end of this dale there is a **lime kiln** on the left and soon the path reaches a road. Turn left for about 50 m then right, off the road and carefully spot the stiles through fields to another road, which is **Cliff Lane**. Turn left and about 100 m on is a seat and four stone troughs (lunch?). Here, leave the road on the left up the path that runs left of a small quarry and to a stile and open fields. The **cave carvings** are at the foot of the small crag on the hillside to the right (no right of way to crag). However, we head over fields towards the left end of a small plantation, where another stile leads to a track and **Rock Farm**. Walk past the farm to a road. Turn left and after about 100 m, turn right on to a path which soon

becomes indistinct but generally follows a line of pylons down a long field. As the pylons veer right, keep ahead and just right of a line of trees to a stile and then another at a farm track. Turn right, cross **Rowlow Brook (Peace Stone)** and then soon left over a wall stile. Follow this stream to a stile on the left, not the woodland gate ahead. Turn right over the stile up to an inscribed circular inset stone **feature** then on to a road. Cross, and walk up the track ahead which leads to **Mount Pleasant Farm**. Leave the drive as it swings left to the farm and turn right to a gate. The track ahead leads above **Kenslow Wood**. Further on a signpost points left to "**Kenslow Knoll** Only". Walk up the field and over a stile to the toposcope and sundial. Return the same way and where the track bears right to Kenslow Farm, turn left over fields and stiles to a road. Turn left and follow the road (where there are grass verges of sorts) back to the car park.

The toposcope at the summit of Kenslow Knoll was embedded in locally quarried stone.

48 Giddy Edge (High Tor), Jug Holes Mine and Oker Hill

Oker and Darley Dale from the summit of Oker Hill (July 29)

One for the family! Catch trains (one steam) from Darley Dale to Matlock Bath; climb High Tor for the views and descend via Giddy Edge; cross the gorge by cable car to the Heights of Abraham with its attractions and, after exiting the Great Masson Cavern, walk back via a short section of the Limestone Way, Jug Holes Mine, Snitterton and Oker Hill.

Length 7 kms/4.4 miles **Map** O/S Explorer OL 24, *White Peak Area*, East Sheet
Start/Finish Peak Rail car park, Station Road, Darley Dale. On B5057 at SK 272 626
Peak Rail and the cable cars are both operative between April and October. A Saturday morning is best. First steam train leaves Darley Dale at 11.35, arrives Matlock Riverside at 11.45. You then have to walk a little to Matlock mainline station for a connection to Matlock Bath. One leaves at 12.39. You could also travel by bus from Darley Dale direct to Matlock Bath. The bus stop is at the chemists on the A6 (see sketch map). The 6.1 service runs regularly. Ask for the cable cars. Or, you could take the steam train to Matlock and then a bus to Matlock Bath! Ring for up to date times : *Peak Rail* : 01629 580381. *Bus Travel-line* : 0870 6082608. *Central Trains* : 0121 634 2040. Public transport leaflets available locally. Matlock bus station is due to be relocated.
Terrain Paths and tracks, some over farmland. Some roadwork. Falls from the top of High Tor (70 metres) or from Giddy Edge would be fatal. Watch the kids and pets.
Refreshments Heights of Abraham (pricey); Matlock Bath or pubs near end of walk.
When To Go/What's There Path to High Tor is immediately right of cable-car ticket kiosk. Descend Giddy Edge on the way back (signs). Cable car station approached from Matlock Bath rail station (signs). Good views from the Victoria Prospect Tower at Heights of Abraham/many other attractions, but leave the Great Masson Cavern until last. Elizabethan Snitterton Hall is one of few Grade 1 listed buildings in Derbyshire. **Nearby** There are sarcophagi and a 2,000 year old yew in St Helen's churchyard, Darley Dale.

228

Above. *Will Shore's Tree above the trig pillar on Oker Hill (Oct 10). The legend of the solitary sycamore spawned Wordsworth's sonnet about two brothers, "The Keepsake".*

Above. *Watching the cable cars from Giddy Edge (July 29). Gulliver's Kingdom theme park (pre-teens) is beyond the cableway and has its own téléphérique.*

Peak Rail occasionally has a guest diesel or steam locomotive such as "Black Prince" and, "Flying Scotsman", seen here drifting through Darley Dale (July 29).

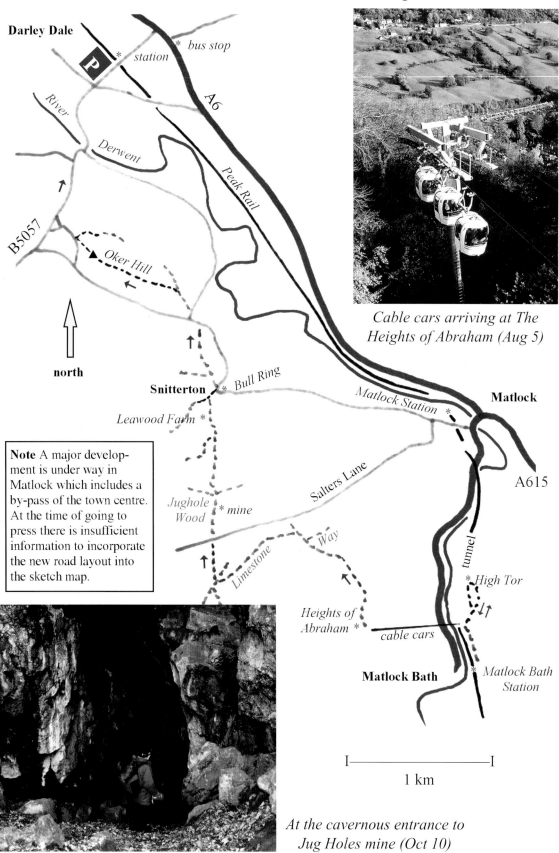

Darley Dale

P * station * bus stop

A6

River

Derwent

Peak Rail

B5057

▲ Oker Hill

north

Snitterton * Bull Ring

Leawood Farm *

Matlock Station *

Matlock

A615

Salters Lane

Note A major development is under way in Matlock which includes a by-pass of the town centre. At the time of going to press there is insufficient information to incorporate the new road layout into the sketch map.

Jughole Wood * mine

Limestone Way

tunnel

* *High Tor*

Heights of Abraham *

cable cars

Matlock Bath * *Matlock Bath Station*

I——————————I
1 km

Cable cars arriving at The Heights of Abraham (Aug 5)

At the cavernous entrance to Jug Holes mine (Oct 10)

Route The route starts at the exit to the Great Masson Cavern. Turn left out of the cavern and follow the path a short distance uphill to the viewing platform (views to **High Tor** and Riber Castle). A few metres above the platform is a track. Turn right and follow the track for about ¾ km to where the **Limestone Way** crosses the track. At the time of writing, there is a seat (*Geoff's*) and a gated stile on the left. Here, turn left off the track and follow the path uphill to another track. Cross, and go ahead through fields via conspicuous stiles, passing a barn on the right, to yet another track. Go through the partially concealed (but waymarked) stile ahead and over more fields to a minor road (**Salters Lane**). Cross, and the path ahead leads across a field to **Jughole Wood**. Descend the path through the wood, ignore a stile on the left, but note and keep well clear of the shafts on the right, to a prominent spoil heap. Here, the path bears right to the cavernous entrance to Jug Holes **mine** (have a look but don't enter). The way leads down left of the spoil heap (ignore another stile on the left) to a gate and onwards to **Leawood Farm**. As you walk down the drive to the right of the farm, you should glimpse the enchanting Snitterton Hall on the left. The drive joins another and then a minor road at **Snitterton**. Here, on the right, is the **Bull Ring** and, on the left, a signed footpath to *Wensley* leads to a three-way sign. Follow the *Oker* direction across fields to a road. Turn left and then right up Aston Lane. After about 30 metres, go through the stile on the left and slant right, uphill (keep the pine trees on your left) and aim for the middle of woodland at the top of the field. Follow the path through the hawthorns to steps and join a path coming up from the left. Turn right on this path and, after about 20 metres, leave it on the left to ascend on another path to a waymarked post and the start of the ridge up **Oker Hill**. Turn right, up the ridge towards the visible landmark of Will Shore's Tree, and beyond to a trig pillar. Ignore any paths that leave the concessionary path over the ridge. Onwards from the pillar, descend to a gate. Turn left then immediately right on the minor road that leads to the **B5057**. Here, turn right and follow the road downhill. Pass the *Three Stags' Heads*; cross the bridge over the **River Derwent**; pass *The Square and Compass* and then Darley Dale Cricket Club on the left, where there is a dated foundation stone in the wall. On the opposite side of the road, columns in the wall allow floodwater to escape. Ahead is Darley Dale railway **station**.

Peak Rail's "Royal Pioneer" approaches Darley Dale from Rowsley (Oct 10).

49 Carsington Water, Harboro' Rocks and Brassington Fields

Carsington Water from the way up to the King's Chair (July 17)

This delightful outing to dolomite limestone outcrops meanders through countryside steeped in ancient history. Maturing Carsington Water has now blended into the landscape and enhances the views from the King's Chair and popular Harboro' Rocks.

Length 11 kms/6.9 miles **Map** O/S Explorer OL 24, *White Peak Area*, East Sheet
Start/Finish Carsington Water (Sheepwash) car park off the B5035 at SK 249 529
Terrain Easy route-finding on farmland paths; a cinder track and a little roadwork.
Refreshments Pubs in Brassington and Carsington.
When To Go/What's There Go in May /Early June when the fields around Brassington and Carsington are carpeted with buttercups and daisies. Mine-spoil grows spring sandwort, mountain pansy, milkwort and thyme. Yellow rattle, cowslips and orchids are followed by harebells, scabious, knapweed and hawkweeds. The pond near Rainster supports yellow flag, bulrush, frogs and dragonflies. Any number of waterfowl may be on Carsington Water, but great-crested grebe and widgeon seem to be always present. A few damselflies are now colonising the marshy margins, and waders such as snipe and redshank also visit. A long-eared owl currently dozes near the car park, where there are bird hides. Buzzards now circle above Harboro' Rocks, where Romano-British remains were found in the cave. The conical Wrekin hill can be seen from the trig pillar (bearing 248°) on a clear day. *The Armchair*, a weathered rock is nearby and the *King's Chair* is a rock resembling a throne. There are medieval ridge and furrow fields and settlement evidence near Rainster Rocks, where skylarks sing. **Nearby** Don't miss Carsington Water Visitor Centre and public hide with CCTV on nesting and waterside birds. Take binoculars. Other refreshments and *The Kugel* are here, too. One kilometre away, human remains in Owslow Cave (fossilised skulls etc) were excavated by C4s *Time Team*.

Quintessential England from the path to Carsington (May 29)

Harboro' Rocks are used by instructors to teach young people climbing and abseiling skills. There are interesting plants, including club-mosses, here, too (May 29).

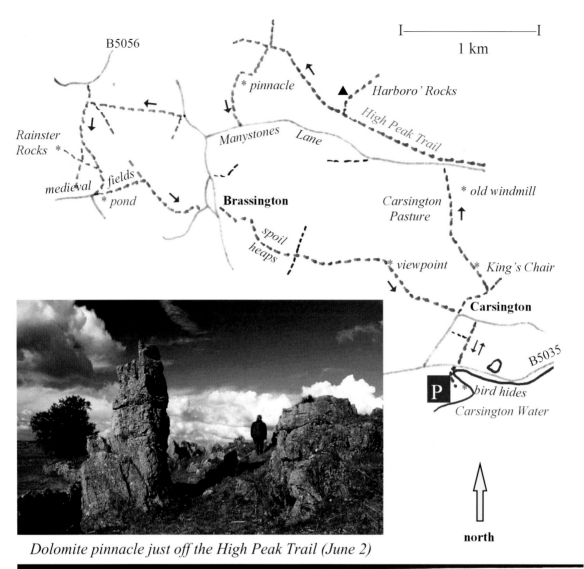

B5056

* pinnacle

▲ Harboro' Rocks

High Peak Trail

Rainster Rocks *

Manystones Lane

medieval fields

* pond

Brassington

spoil heaps

Carsington Pasture

* old windmill

* viewpoint

* King's Chair

Carsington

B5035

P * bird hides

Carsington Water

I————————I
1 km

north

Dolomite pinnacle just off the High Peak Trail (June 2)

Bird-watching on Carsington Water from the Paul Stanley Hide at the start of the walk.

Route In the CP, face the reservoir and turn left; pass the wood sculpture on your left and immediately turn right. Signposted off this path are two public bird hides, both worth a visit. After these, the path rounds a narrow arm of **Carsington Water** en route to the **B5035**. Cross the road (with care) and go up the track, which soon drops down to **Carsington**. Pub ahead but turn left, pass cross stump/seats on right, then join minor road and, after about 70 metres, turn right up the FP (concealed sign to *Ible* and *Grangemill*). The way leads between houses and a leafy tunnel before emerging at the bottom of the hillside up to the **King's Chair**, which is reached after turning left at the wall at the top. The way ahead meanders over **Carsington Pasture** to a road. Cross, and two stiles later bear left along the cinder track of the **High Peak Trail**. A fast km brings the footpath on the right to **Harboro' Rocks**. The cave is at the left of the crags. Return to track. About ¾ km on, turn left at X-paths. Go up the fields, bear right then left (outcrops on left) and descend to a farm and its track, which leads to a road, **Manystones Lane**. Turn right and right again at the junction and, 300 metres on, turn left off the road at a twin finger-post. Go straight ahead through a number of breached walls and fields to the right of a barn, where there is a stile/gate. Turn right then sharp left (keep wall on left), follow the path down past **Rainster Rocks** to the right and past a gate on the left before reaching a tight squeezer stile on the left before a prominent outcrop. Keep right of the outcrop, cross **medieval fields** to emerge at the start of a track at a road bend. Turn left to the end of the track then go right through fields which lead down to **Brassington**. Go left on the road then right, down the path through the churchyard. Turn left on the road which bends right, past the *Miners Arms* to a road junction. Ahead, up to the left of *Waverley House*, a path leads between buildings to a stile. The route is now easy to follow as the path heads first uphill and then bears 90° right to undulate over fields (spoil heaps), crosses a track and leads back to Carsington.

The buttercup fields and mine-spoil hummocks above Brassington (May 29)

The footpath to Crich Stand crosses the tram terminus (Sept 6)

A walk full of variety that initially rises through woodland to Crich Stand tower; visits the village of Crich for an optional tram ride and/or lunch at "Cardale" Fish Restaurant, before descending through woodland, to a towpath walk through a local nature reserve.

Length 11 kms/6.9 miles **Map** O/S Explorer OL 24, *White Peak Area*, East Sheet
Start/Finish Whatstandwell Station car park, off the A6 at SK 333 541
Terrain Easy to follow paths and tracks, some muddy after rain. Some roads/lanes.
Refreshments *Derwent Hotel* near car park. Pubs, cafés, chips and shops in Crich.
When To Go/What's There To ascend Crich Stand (50 steps) for the views (10p fee), go on a summer Saturday or Sunday otherwise it may be locked. Millennium beacon and info boards here plus memorabilia in the tea rooms. Crich was the original *Cardale* in ITV's *Peak Practice* (until it relocated to Ashover). Whilst in Crich, why not treat the kids (or yourselves) to a tram ride at Crich Tramway Village (01773 852565). *The Green Man* by Andrew Frost and *The Lead Miners* by Lorraine Botterill are among sculptures in the grounds. In late spring and summer, the hoverflies, dragonflies and damselflies are at their best on the canal. Pike, bream, water-plantain, pondweeds and hornwort can be seen in the canal and, little grebe, kingfisher, hawfinch, grass snake, slow worm and water vole are there for early, quiet visitors. Waterside plants include flowering-rush, hemp agrimony, water figwort, reed sweet-grass, arrowhead, branched bur-reed, tansy and skullcap. Frog and bee orchids, together with spring sandwort and perforate St. John'swort, flower on the quarry spoil-heaps. Butterflies en route include holly blue, speckled wood, gatekeeper, large skipper and small copper. Whatstandwell Station footbridge was built by world-renowned bridge-builder Andrew Handyside. **Nearby** Lea Gardens (SK 323 572) are a blaze of colour at azalea time, May /early June. The Alport Stone (p.21) is worth a visit (brave graffiti!), and restored Heage Windmill near Belper sails again!

Top Left. *Crich Church (May 13)*

Top Right. *Crich village cross unusually includes a boy on one face (May 13)*

Bottom Left. *Bluebell glade with red campion beside the Cromford Canal (May 13)*

Bottom Right. *"Cardale" lived on at the fish and chip restaurant in Crich! (May 13)*

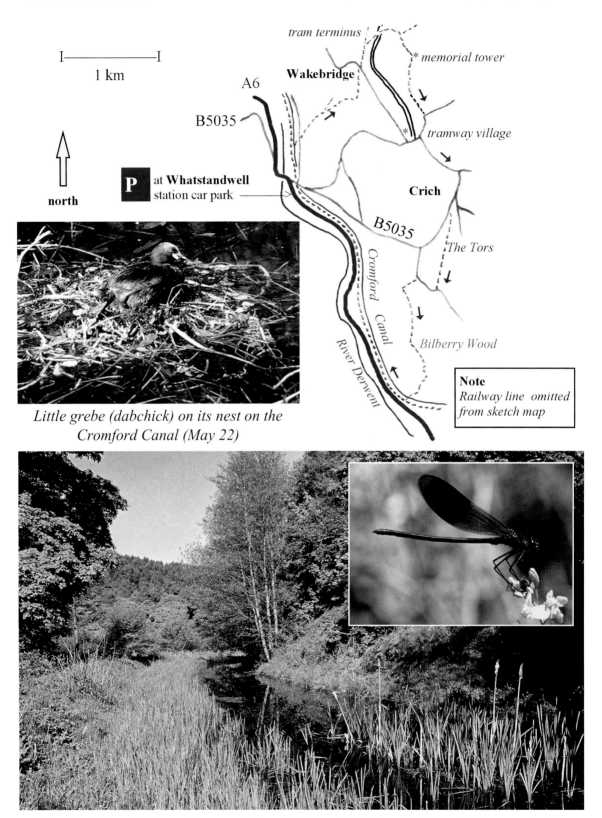

I——————I
1 km

↑
north

P at **Whatstandwell** station car park

tram terminus

Wakebridge

A6

B5035

* *memorial tower*

* *tramway village*

Crich

B5035

The Tors

Cromford Canal

River Derwent

Bilberry Wood

Note
Railway line omitted from sketch map

Little grebe (dabchick) on its nest on the Cromford Canal (May 22)

Cromford Canal Nature Reserve (May 22). **Inset.** *The banded demoiselle, rare in The Peak, hunts at the Cromford Canal but breeds in the adjacent River Derwent (June 28).*

Route Cross the railway line via the footbridge and then turn right at steps to the **Cromford Canal** (sign to *Derwent Valley Heritage Way*). Turn left at the towpath, walk under a road bridge and, after about 300 metres, cross the canal via a footbridge (sign to *Wakebridge*). Soon after, take the left fork of the path and follow it up through woodland; cross a minor road and continue upwards, passing old quarries (with climbing potential) on the right. Keep ahead after crossing a stream (ignore stile on left), and go over the stile into a field then more woodland. Another stile leads to open ground where, later, the paths swings left to a road at **Wakebridge**. Turn right then immediately left up a track (sign to *Plaistow Green*). Keep ahead, ignore stile on left, to reach the **tram terminus**. Cross the line and bear right at a path junction above Cliff Quarry to reach the **Memorial Tower** at Crich Stand. Turn right onto the road at the bottom of the entrance lane to the tower (care, no path). This leads to Cromford Road on the left. (Here, keep ahead to the **Tramway Village** on the right, if you opt for a visit). Turn left down Cromford Road, pass the church and bear right at the village cross onto the **B5035**. Walk downhill, pass the *Black Swan* on the left to reach **Crich** Market Square (*Cardale Fish Bar* on left). Keep on the B5035 (sign to *Wirksworth*) and walk up Sandy Lane. Opposite the Fire Station, take the footpath which is signed to *Chadwick Nick*. This leads south through fields and stiles across **The Tors** and down steps to a minor road. Turn right (care, no footpath) for about 250 metres, then take the footpath on the left through fields. At a stile, the path turns 90° left and starts its descent through the trees and clearings of **Bilberry Wood**. There are waymark signs, but not one at a junction, where a tempting wide path proceeds left. Here, the footpath itself leads ahead and down to eventually arrive at a gate, left of a bridge over the canal. Cross the bridge, turn right onto the towpath, and follow it 3 kms north(ish) to the car park.

The Sherwood Foresters' memorial tower at Crich Stand (May 22)

"The Big Walk" - a traverse of the Peak District from north to south

Looking to Higher and Lower Shelf Stones on Bleaklow from The Pennine Way (Dec 8)

This epic journey through the Peak District National Park was devised by Tony Gibbs, Roger Wright and Roger Yarwood, who worked together at the Peak Park Planning Board. Known to its masochistic followers as "The Big Walk", the object was to walk from north to south through the entire National Park in under 24 hours. It was not to be a race, rather a social outing, with regular stops where refreshments could be bought - so less to carry. 1969 saw the first success - the group collapsing over the finishing line with 20 minutes to spare! These days it has been marched and run in half the time, but the spirit of the original pioneers lives on, and every year a group sets off with similar ideals.

The group usually sets off from Marsden at 05.30 hrs on the Saturday nearest to the longest day; has breakfast at Crowden Youth Hostel (book beforehand 01457 852135); lunches at The Snake Inn, Woodlands Valley; has tea at Edale café; supper at Anglers' Rest at Millers Dale and a final pint at the Bull i'th'Thorn on the A515. **A few tips** : arrange a lift home from Thorpe; petroleum jelly on your feet/ankles will greatly reduce the risk of blisters, but do take a first aid/blister kit; carry torch/headlamp with spare battery for the final leg in the dark; travel light - water bottles can be refilled at the stops; a mobile phone could enable early retirees to phone for a lift, but there are public phones at the refreshment points; take sufficient money and be skilled in map/compass.

Basic Route: (you require OL21 for the first mile or so). Start: Marsden (at 048 112) via Butterley Reservoir to Wessenden Head (076 072); Black Hill summit to Crowden YH (11 miles); Bleaklow Head to Snake Inn (20 miles); Seal Stones, Kinder to Edale (25 miles); Mam Nick (125 835) to point 130 800 (change to *White Peak* map) - Anglers' Rest (142 733 at 35 miles); Bull i'th'Thorn (41 miles) to Hartington (46 miles); Beresford Dale, Wolfscote Dale, Dovedale and Lin Dale to the park boundary, just south of Thorpe (164 488, *Explorer* 259). **Total** 57 miles, but must be 60 after meanderings!

Some Other Peak Attractions

Lumsdale Waterfall (SK 313 606) is not marked on the White Peak map. Here, the falls leap 20 metres down a tiny grit gorge, and a short walk could also include mill remains and, over the road, the *Wishing Stone* and an ancient flight of steps beneath a tunnel of ivy.

Waterfall Swallet (SK 198 770) again, not marked on map as a waterfall, is a secluded fall into a wooded, limestone ravine. In the ravine is a low, narrow cave entrance. This is a Grade 4 from which rescue would be impossible. Under no circumstances enter the cave.

Lumsdale falls

Robin Hood's Picking Rods (or The Maiden Stones) SK 005 909, are a pair of pillars embedded in stone, whose origin remains a mystery, although legends and theories abound. A walk could start from Charlesworth and also include Coombes Tor and Rocks.

White Nancy

White Nancy is a huge, bell-shaped monument on the Saddle of Kerridge overlooking Bollington at SJ 939 771. Extensive views include Manchester airport. Create your own circular walk starting from Lamaload Reservoir! (Car park at SJ 975 752).

Bar Brook stone circle (SK 278 755) could be included in a walk starting from Shillito Wood CP and nearby cross (SK 295 748) to Greave's Piece and back via Barbrook Little Reservoir and Ramsley Moor - adder country! (The second of my 4 bites!!).

Black Rocks picnic site (SK 292 557) has a short orienteering course through nearby woods. Map from Middleton Top Visitor Centre, which houses the old engine house for the Cromford Incline (part of *High Peak Trail*). The National Stone Centre is nearby.

Edale has become famous as the starting (or finishing) post for the *Pennine Way*, the first long distance path, which was formally opened in 1965. The busy hamlet also boasts a fine old bridge, campsite and the *Nags Head*. Do visit *The Moorland Centre* at Fieldhead.

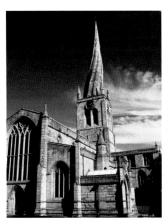

Chesterfield's icon

Holmfirth boasts *Last of The Summer Wine* locations and an exhibition. Nearby are fine walks from Ramsden Reservoir (CP at SE 115 056) to Elysium (an earthly farm) and Hades (with its name dry-stone walled) or further afield to Cook's Study Hill.

Chesterfield, just to the east of The Peak, is a much improved mining town which retains some of its character: a Thursday flea market on the cobblestones; museum and information centre and, for wet days with the kids, swimming pool with flume; multiplex cinema; amusements and ten-pin bowling. The *Pomegranate Theatre* presents plays etc, the *Winding Wheel* shows etc and, of course, there is *that* spire. Can be intimidating at night.

Bakewell (left) was once a bustling but charming market town, which has been considerably "developed" in recent years. A plethora of retail outlets and an outrageous eyesore for an agriculture centre, which can be seen from all the surrounding hills, are now what the town portrays. What the National Park Authority was thinking of was anyone's guess. As endless shoppers ply food detritus to the gorging mallards on the R. Wye, so too come the scavengers - and black-headed gull, Muscovy duck and Canada goose now add to the eutrophication of the river. But it's not all doom and gloom: Bakewell's carnival is by far the best in The Peak (first Saturday in July); there is a fine packhorse bridge near Holme Hall; an annual show; vintage motorbike museum; and you could always send one of those puddings to someone you're not too keen on …

Buxton has an Opera House, Pavilion (tropical plants) and many other fine buildings built using profits from Ecton Copper Mines. There is a swimming pool, museum, Poole's Cavern with walk up to Grinlow Tower and a fountain of free mineral water!

Rivelin Rocks and Needle in the east of The Peak (SK 277 872), together with Rivelin dams and Wyming Brook, provide popular walks for people from the Sheffield area.

Roystone Rocks (SK 197 568) are groups of weathered dolomite limestone rocks on a barrow hill. Now on access land (stile 199 569), these unusual outcrops are well worth a visit and can be included in a walk that encompasses the chambered barrow of Minninglow and the medieval monastic farm of Roystone Grange. This area is an archaeologists paradise, with Romano–British settlements, Bronze Age cemeteries and Roman wall and road remains. Minninglow Car Park is at SK 194 581.

Roystone Rocks (May 23)

Looking into lower Ramsden Clough (Aug 17)

Ramsden Clough (SE 119 035) was "pirated" by walkers for years - determined not to be denied this wild and wonderful cleft to the south of Holmbridge. Tenuous access proposals permit a visit to the head of the clough, which is best reached by walking east from the viewpoint car park at Holme Moss (SE 097 038). To make a wild day of it, head south from the CP into Heyden Brook, cross the A6024, round Dewhill Naze and battle on to the clough!

Bibliography/Further Reading

There is, of course, a plethora of walking guide books to The Peak - far too many to mention here. However, I list some other publications which may be of interest. Those out of print should be available from libraries or perhaps local second-hand book shops :

Archaeology in the Peak District by D. Bramwell (Moorland, 1973)
Curiosities of Derbyshire by F. Rodgers (Derbyshire Countryside, 1992)
Dark Peak Aircraft Wrecks Vol. 1 by R. Collier & R. Wilkinson (Leo Cooper, 1997)
Dark Peak Aircraft Wrecks Vol. 2 by R. Collier (Leo Cooper, 1998)
Geology Explained in the Peak District by F. W. Cope (David & Charles, 1976)
Industrial Archaeology of the Peak District by H. Harris (David & Charles, 1971)
More Curiosities of Derbyshire by F. Rodgers (Derbyshire Countryside, 2000)
Peak Villages by K. Frenkel & R. Smith (Halsgrove, 2002)
Peakland Roads & Trackways by A.E. & E.M. Dodd (Landmark, 2004)
Supernatural Peak District by D. Clarke (Robert Hale, 2000)
The King's England, Derbyshire etc by A. Mee (King's England Press, 1990)
The Nature of Derbyshire ed. by T. Elkinton (Barracuda, 1986)
The Peak District by M.J.B. Baddeley (Ward, Lock & Co, 1937)
The Peak District by R. Christian (David & Charles, 1976)
The Peak District by R. Millward & A. Robinson (Eyre Methuen, 1975)
Wild Flowers etc of the Peak District by P. Anderson & D. Shimwell (Moorland, 1981)
Wild Peak by M. Hamblin (Halsgrove, 2003)
Upper Derwent, 10,000 years of History by B. Bevan (Tempus, 2004)

*Annually, The Peak National Park Authority publishes a free official newspaper and guide to The Peak. As well as announcing events by month, it lists places of interest, Tourist Information Centres etc which, in turn, can provide campsites, youth hostels etc. Some addresses that may not be included are:

Challenge The Peak, Outdoor Pursuits Instruction, 48 Farfield Road, Herringthorpe, Rotherham, S. Yorks S65 3DH. (Glyn Brown 01709 328828)

Whitehall Outdoor Pursuits Centre, Long Hill, Buxton, Derbyshire (01298 23260)

Edale Mountain Rescue Team PO Box 6490, Bakewell, Derbyshire DE45 1XR. Web : www.edalemountainrescue.co.uk All mountain rescue and cave rescue teams are tireless volunteers. Support them!

Acknowledgements

I would like to thank (in no order) : Derek Whiteley for determining the long-eared bat; Stan Dobson for determining the cave spider; Martin Coleman for providing information on the Peak Tor earthwork; the gift shops in Castleton for permitting me to photograph their Blue John; Steve Newell for saying "It's about time you wrote one, not bought another"; Pete Woolhouse for proof-reading the script and sharing many wonderful days in The Peak, and my family; wife Brenda, son Reece and daughter Susie, who walked in all weather without complaint. Dave Mitchell, David Booker and Guy at Scarthin Books were very supportive. Dents and Jessops, both of Chesterfield, scanned the slides to CD. Brenda "burnt" my *Publisher* files to CD; Susie converted them to PDF and Reece's IT skills saved the book more than once. It has to be said, that without the support of my family and Pete, I may well have faltered. Thus, with thanks, I dedicate this book to them.

Rod Dunn has been walking, climbing and conducting environmental surveys in The Peak District for over 30 years. He has also climbed extensively in the Alps, Dolomites and Tyrol and ascended all the major European peaks. In 1969 he was in the first party to successfully walk the Peak District National Park from north to south in under 24 hours. In 1982 he co-founded *The British Dragonfly Society* and in 1984 *Derbyshire Dragonflies* was published. His 24-year survey of dragonflies in Derbyshire was published in 2005. His photographs appear in the local and national press and many wildlife publications. An anthology of his illustrated verse, *Aerosol Dreams*, was published in 1975. For many seasons he played football for Bakewell and Tideswell. His roots are firmly in the Peak District: his mother's line descends from the *Fox House Inn* near Grindleford, and his father's from the *Belle Vue Hotel*, Tideswell (now a private residence). Born in Bakewell, he was educated at Lady Manners and lives in Darley Dale.

The photographs were taken on a Canon AE-1 fitted with a 28 mm Tamron lens (until dropped once too often) and then a Nikon F65 fitted with a Nikkar 28-80 zoom lens. The few shots that include myself were taken using a tripod and self-timer - the remainder were taken without a tripod. Most photos are dated to give an indication of what's around then; but a photo captures a moment of time or nature that can never be repeated. Film was largely Fujichrome Sensia 100, with the occasional Kodachrome 64 used for winter. The photographs were all taken during normal "walking hours", hence there are no sunrises or sunsets. Falls of water were not "accelerated" as our eyes never see this manipulation.

The author summits the Matterhorn in the autumn of 1968. Note the dangerous chest harness, basic equipment and inadequate clothing compared to today's hi-tec gear!
(photo credit Hans 'Bodo' Altmann)